DARK PSYCHOLOGY

Discover All Deception Tactics Used by Manipulators

(Discover How to Influence People in an Ethical Way by Learning the Secrets)

Charles Walton

Published By Regina Loviusher

Charles Walton

All Rights Reserved

Dark Psychology: Discover All Deception Tactics Used by Manipulators (Discover How to Influence People in an Ethical Way by Learning the Secrets)

ISBN 978-1-77485-298-9

All rights reserved. No part of this guide may be reproduced in any form without permission in writing from the publisher except in the case of brief quotations embodied in critical articles or reviews.

Legal & Disclaimer

The information contained in this book is not designed to replace or take the place of any form of medicine or professional medical advice. The information in this book has been provided for educational and entertainment purposes only.

The information contained in this book has been compiled from sources deemed reliable, and it is accurate to the best of the Author's knowledge; however, the Author cannot guarantee its accuracy and validity and cannot be held liable for any errors or omissions. Changes are periodically made to this book. You must consult your doctor or get professional medical advice before using any of the suggested remedies, techniques, or information in this book.

Upon using the information contained in this book, you agree to hold harmless the Author from and against any damages, costs, and expenses, including any legal fees potentially resulting from the application of any of the information provided by this guide. This disclaimer applies to any damages or injury caused by the use and application, whether directly or indirectly, of any advice or information presented, whether for breach of contract, tort, negligence, personal injury, criminal intent, or under any other cause of action.

You agree to accept all risks of using the information presented inside this book. You need to consult a professional medical practitioner in order to ensure you are both able and healthy enough to participate in this program.

TABLE OF CONTENTS

INTRODUCTION 1

CHAPTER 1: WHAT TO UTILIZE NLP TO CONTROL EMOTIONS 7

CHAPTER 2: MAKING-UP OF A MANIPULATOR 30

CHAPTER 3: WHO USES DARK PSYCHOLOGY? 49

CHAPTER 4: WHAT YOU CAN DO TO BE SAFE FROM MANIPULATION 58

CHAPTER 5: THE DIFFERENT TYPES OF MANIPULATION ... 70

CHAPTER 6: WHAT IS INFLUENCE AND PERSUASION? 85

CHAPTER 7: A COMPREHENSIVE STUDY OF MANIPULATION 97

CHAPTER 8: DARK PERSUASION METHODS 105

CHAPTER 9: HOW TO USE NEURO-LINGUISTIC PROGRAMMING "MANIPULATE" THE MIND 124

CHAPTER 10: PSYCHOLOGY OF MANIPULATION 131

CHAPTER 11: DECEPTION TACTICS 149

CHAPTER 12: LEARN TO UNDERSTAND THE 4 PERSONALITY QUALITIES IN THE DARK TRIAD 170

CONCLUSION 185

Introduction

Manipulation is the art of convincing someone to do something you would like them to in a way that they would not do if you directly asked. Like all art forms it could be learned or developed through repetition.

Although manipulation can involve the use of deceit but it doesn't necessarily mean that the manipulator is seeking to harm their victim. The majority of the time, they simply want to influence the target for profit, whether that's emotional physically, financially, or sexually.

While the word "manipulation" has an unpopular negative connotation and stigma, we're all guilty of manipulating others. This doesn't necessarily mean that we don't get along It's just a matter of control and power.

Persuasion is thought of as an influence technique that is soft which is utilized in sales, politics, negotiations, and relationships as well as when dealing with others. It is, therefore, extremely beneficial. The most basic ability manipulators have can be the capacity to discern other people's mental and emotional states.

Expert manipulators know how to fool people by understanding the psychological weaknesses that their targets suffer. They accomplish this by hiding their true motives. They are able to select the best manipulative strategy to cover every weakness they reveal. In this book, you'll be taught how to do this!

We believe that manipulators should have some degree of ruthlessness, and feel guilty for the hurt they inflict on their victims. This is the image that is painted by films and soap-operas on TV. The reality is that anyone can influence and convince people, including the most nice people you've ever met!

This book will explain how the environment we live in influences our perception of and interpret things. Perhaps you're wondering how you could be influenced by TV shows you are watching? This book will provide the information.

There's also a chapter on Brainwashing which is when a person's beliefs and views regarding something are completely altered through the use of force or systematic methods. This may even happen within our intimate relationships where we're often conditioned to believe that we're not attractive enough, good enough or intelligent enough.

Different techniques of persuasion have been employed throughout through the ages. The well-known 17th-century French philosopher and physicist Blaise Pascal, believed that the most reliable method of convincing someone to take the action you want them to do isn't by inundating them with your thoughts and ideas, but rather by'slipping via the doorway of their convictions'. That is, persuasion by wit and sweetness rather than authority.

Pascal is popular for his thoughts that eloquence is the art of expressing ideas in a way so that the people who hear your words can listen without feeling insulted or ill-treated but be content to consider your thoughts for what they are.

Through the power of influence, the world, we are more effective in our lives, and consequently achieve more of our goals satisfied. First, determine what you're trying to accomplish and then develop the best strategy for how you can achieve it.

If you are regularly engaged in business or difficult negotiations reading people is one of the most valuable abilities. People we interact with every day transmit signals to us that if we discern what we should pay attention to, each person will be able to tell us precisely how we can influence them. Being able to read people's signals is a skill that everyone can learn by paying greater focus. The most effective targets to be manipulated by mind are typically the people who are too sensitive or insensitive.

When we are in the market for something, we typically present our arguments in the hope that the other party is willing to listen to our demands. If we do this it is likely that there will be a chance that they'll say no. With the knowledge provided in this book, you can discover advanced methods of persuasion that are based on psychological loopholes and subconscious influences.

This book will demonstrate the steps to follow in clear and easy-to-follow methods. When we know what motivates humans, it is possible to leverage the basic human need as a way to convince people to say "Yes" frequently to us. You can also discover the most advanced NLP (Neuro-Linguistic programming) methods employed by world-renowned magicians that are now available to those who want to learn. These methods and techniques are designed with care to show you how to get through your day while ensuring that you have all of your requirements met.

Leave your morals to the side since the goal in this text is to expose the dark side of getting what you want.

Chapter 1: What to Utilize NLP To Control Emotions

In NLP there is no such thing such as an ineffective person, but rather an uninspiring state. Being able to manage your state in order to stay innovative even in the most difficult situations is worth a lot in regardless of where you work, no matter what you do and who you are!

Whatever project you're required to complete, or whatever you want the outcome to be, consider "what condition would I like to be in for making this task easy?"

On and when you'd wish to or have to alter your situation in order to help you in performing at your best, there are many ways to accomplish this by using NLP methods.

For starters to get you started, here are three easy strategies to help you in handling your emotional state:

1. The core interest

You can alter the pictures you create for yourself. You can change what you're envisioning, but the way you imagine it. Change the sound you hear, and gradually become more aware and concentrate on the best image. Have you ever seen what happens when you're feeling a bit low or out of sorts and then, your favorite piece of inspirational music? Modify the music and the way you imagine the final product.

2. Physiology

Make your body change dramatically move, do whatever you can to push various synthetic concoctions through your body's sensory system, whether it is doing more exercise or simply using the stairs instead of the lift. Alter your posture Stand tall, tall and powerful, not only will you appear more confident and confident, but you'll feel more confident. Think about changing your appearance, as well as your breathing. Even the smallest of tweaks can help you in managing your mood.

3. Self-Talk

Change the way you talk to yourself or your self-talk. You can alter the content or the tone of your thoughts, and you're your self-made hero. What about changing the inside pundit to show that you're not good enough? Imagine how hilarious you would find it if your inner pundit was voiced by Mickey Mouse or the Donkey from Shrek? Then, change the location of the voices to ensure it comes from your left toe!

Every state is created through the interaction between your thinking patterns as well as your physiology and neurochemicals. Any of these changes can alter your condition.

The ability to alter your situation and decide what you feel about yourself can be one of your skills to live a passionate and joyful life. Passionate opportunity doesn't mean you have to feel depressed, but it means you're constantly aware of negative moods and choose your response.

There are many ways by people can develop the capacity to effectively manage their state. This is just one of the many amazing techniques using NLP to aid you in doing your best in spite of the circumstances that are affecting your life.

Increase your passion for learning by using NLP

As we discover more and more about what constitutes succeed in business, and especially in the field of administration, the assumption is shifting away from typical characteristics of IQ and specialist capacity toward a more enthusiastic approach to understanding. The concept of passion for knowledge is now seen as an "need to be a" fix in the making up of pioneers.

Contrary to our intelligence and our IQ, our enthusiasm can be developed and improved by preparing. NLP Training is a great way to do this. In its Wikipedia description as "the capability to detect and evaluate your own feelings, those of others, and gatherings."

Enthusiastic Intelligence

Five of the components of our skin which we can attribute to our passion for knowledge:

Mindfulness What do we know about our own personal temperaments state of mind, emotions, and states and how they influence our actions? Do we really believe that we're aware of the way our state of mind affect other people? How well would you state you're able to discern your own strengths and flaws, characteristics as well as needs and motivations?

Self-regulation - How good can we claim to be at recognizing our own feelings before we take action? We can confidently affirm that we're able to manage our state of mind and motives to ensure an enviable distance from behavior that has negative implications for us as well as others?

Inspiration - How strong is your desire to continue to pursue your goals? What are your overall energy levels? Do you feel energized to work for a lifetime and do you have a passion that's beyond cash and energy?

Sympathy: How easy can we get to understand another's point of view? What can we learn about the passionate nature of other people? What can we do to adjust our behavior to reflect the opinions of others?

Social Skill - How efficiently would you describe yourself as prepared to build the right kind of affinity and identify common interests so that you can effectively interact with your contacts?

NLP covers every one of these zones . NLP Training is designed to operate at an oblivious level to make sure that as soon when you are aware of what you need to do, you are able to demonstrate proficiency in doing it. It is only through the preparation of conduct for your brain that the behavior becomes consistent and unchanging and is developed through working with the intuitive part of your cerebrum.

NLP enhances enthusiasm for knowledge

What about taking an examination of how NLP can benefit you in by utilizing the five components previously mentioned:

Self Awareness

The NLP Practitioner course, the focus is on developing an understanding of how your cerebrum functions and how you create your interactions and how your behavior develops. This helps you understand the mind-sets, dispositions and states, and then see the ways you've achieved these states and dispositions.

A large portion of NLP Submodalities work is tied to empowering you to modify your thoughts and feelings, as well as your preferences through understanding and regulating the higher-quality factors you consider.

Self-Regulation

NLP Anchoring empowers you to discern and alter your mood in a flash. It also lets you establish triggers that naturally bring a positive vibe within you in specific circumstances. This can be beneficial in instances where you're likely to discover that you are operating with no success previously.

In the Strategies section of NLP's Practitioner course, we will discover why we are prone to certain blind thinking techniques that are the basis of our daily routines. We discover ways to take these systems apart and alter them to produce better behavior in our pursuit of excellence.

Motivation

NLP is all about outcomes. It's all about deciding what you want and how you can improve , and determining the best way that will help you in getting there.

By using NLP Submodalities and Timeline procedures you can make your goals and goals convincing and guide your energy towards achieving them.

Neurological Levels is an element of the NLP Practitioner's preparation and this knowledge empowers you to make sure that you are working, plan and set goals for yourself and others at a level that is logical and lets you achieve whatever goals you might be aiming for.

Empathy

Perceptual positions is a great activity that is taught in the NLP Practitioner program where you can relive an experience from your past. You encountered a problem with correspondence with someone else, and you examine the situation from three divine observers. The scenario is seen from your personal position and the perspective of the other person and also from the position of a flies on the wall. This allows you to begin to build the most of other people and to view things in a different way.

In NLP Sensory Acuity is linked to being able to discern small changes in another which are correlated with what they are thinking. This allows you to discern their moods the changes in their temperament and even their emotions.

The entire course for NLP Master Practitioner preparation is centered around helping you understand the other people and what is important to them. You will discover how to understand your own and other people's esteems and character, in with helping you to most likely alter your working tasks in accordance with their needs and preferences, and to increase the likelihood of advancing them.

Social Skills

NLP provides a method of "getting into Rapport" with another. There's a huge variety of ways you could discover an individual's compatibility and the majority of them are completely unobserved to you, and so you don't even know the method you used to get there. There are instances when you feel an affinity and feel that lively relationship with people, but in some occasions, you do not. NLP Rapport process empowers you to be able to discern what creates the connection and then to create it happen without fail!

NLP helps you create compatibility by combining breath, words you speak as well as the sentences you construct, and how you move your body. This allows people to be more likely to affect other people.

The benefits of creating arousing insight using NLP

There are immediate benefits in using NLP to increase your passion for learning Here is the key point you'll be able to comprehend:

Mindfulness - Greater realness, fearlessness

Self Regulation - More willingness to be honest and open to the possibility of change

Inspiration , optimism, a strong determination to achieve and succeed more, and a higher level of duty

Sympathy - Increased ability to collaborate with others create amazing groups and hold the top people. Amazing interpersonal skills

Social Skills - Greater capacity to influence and persuade others to lead to change.

What exactly is NLP? These four techniques could alter your thinking

Neuro-etymological Programming (NLP) is commonly utilized to enhance the quality of relationships. Additionally, it can be utilized for self-awareness as well as improvement. Some NLP techniques can help you live a more attractive and vital life.

In reality, NLP underscores the significance of mastering higher-mindfulness strategies to identify instances, thoughts and skepticisms that could keep you from experiencing happiness within your own life. Below are four key NLP techniques you can use and the research behind them.

1. Mooring

Mooring is one of the most popular NLP techniques. The goal is to create positive reactions by inviting the other person to with a particular mental and emotional state of mind to a grapple which could be a visual or word or a movement. A tightening of the belt improves our ability to manage emotions and be able to perform a job of self-management which makes us less prone to feel weak and overwhelmed.

Step-by-step instructions on how for using the mooring process

*Recall when you experienced an extreme positive emotion that you want to activate in various situations (for example , feeling satisfied when you have achieved an improvement).

Bring in tactile signals that correspond to the state (for example , what you felt feel, smelled or felt, or heard).

*Bring your memory to its highest point, and then you can join your emotions for remain (for instance, put a ring in your

finger, then squeeze your cartilage of your ear).

*Take a short break and repeat the steps in the previous.

Test the stay (for example , you can squeeze on your cartilage in the middle of your ear) to generate the unique feeling of achievement.

You would then be able use this technique at any time you require an enthusiastic lift me-up. It can be used together or in conjunction with other NLP methods.

Securing is based on the notion of molding, in which upgrading triggers specific reactions. The process of tying down triggers the response you require to trigger the reaction through the repetition of. It can benefit you by making you in the position of being accountable for your emotions. Additionally, some studies suggest that when paired with various methods and prayers Securing can help you overcome anxiety and silly feelings of fear and anxiety.

2. Reframing

The next item in the list of NLP methods is reframing or re-examining unpleasant events by using an alternative outline. This lets you allow your mind to be open to situations that could be in the future, as opposed to insisting on negatives. Simply put reframing shifts the focus from overwhelming and negative positive and empowered.

The most efficient method to change the way you frame an concept, emotion or behavior:

* Identify the feeling, idea or behaviour you wish to change.

Establish contact with the most numbing part of you that is triggering the negative mental state. This could be a image or voice, or an articulated voice, etc.

Find the positive motive in that sentence. Imagine you're scared of flying. The noise of a plane's motor starting to take off creates tension because it is supposed to ensure that you are safe. This is a great goal but the response is not there.

Focusing on the positive outcome and experimenting with a variety of methods of reactivity that help you to recognize this purpose. Take for example, recognizing the confidence and self-defense, that's why you choose the safest method of travel (flying instead of driving).

Make sure your intuition is focused on attempting to make the possibility of elective reactions and it doesn't hinder your reframing efforts. Be aware of any conflicting beliefs, and if you find yourself rationalizing you can go back to step four to discover alternative methods of reacting.

Reframing can be used as an approach to restorative therapy due to its capacity to modify perceptions. Different parts of the cerebrum stimulate memories and emotions memories are stored in the hippocampus, whereas the amygdala controls emotions.

In the course of reviewing previous events the amygdala responds by triggering a sensation similar to the one that was first felt but reframing the situation helps us realize that it is the nature of our brains to recognize that the feeling doesn't have to be fixed and we are able to dismantle the patterns of programming and arrange the sound reaction over automated responses. Reframing is one of the NLP methods that prove that it is possible to free yourself from the amygdala's purported grasp.

3. Meta-demonstrating

Meta-demonstrating is among the most prevalent NLP methods due to its ability to identify intentional limitations that may keep you from reaching the bliss. The easiest way to meta-model is to take look at the language you employ in your everyday life, and focusing on these three kinds of instances:

Generalisations, proves in considerations in the form of "I'm generally so unlucky" as well as "all men are alike."

Mind wandering (for instance "John did not like me this afternoon, he ought to be furious by my behavior") or causes-impact articulated statements (for instance "in the event that I fail to become more fit I'll feel as an unfulfilled person").

*Deletes, or carefully determining your perception of reality in order to support your prior beliefs. For instance, someone who has low confidence might ignore compliments and devote too much time to look at things, leading to thoughts such as "individuals do not find me attractive."

Instructions for using meta-demonstrating: Consider which category your thoughts are in the class, and then start an investigation process to examine the non-adaptive design. For instance If you are in a position of "individuals do not consider me attractive" Meta-demonstrating questions to inquire about are "which people specifically?" and "how do you know this?".

It is likely that your responses will include an unison statement that includes "consistently" or "never" "consistently" as well as "never" At the point you have an chance to think about whether you're justified in declaring that everything is in this manner and never this way. If you are meta-displaying, it is useful to find out on alternative approaches. For example, in the statement "in the case that I don't become more fit, I'll feel as being disappointed" Consider asking yourself if the event that feeling like that feeling of disappointment is your only option.

Meta-displaying can be a powerful tool because it requires users to question imbued reaction models that may be transformed into what experts in cognitive science refer to as excessive shirking behaviour that limits your ability to learn from new experiences. The efficacy of this process is also related to the concept division. If we compare it against a different scenario it is possible to be able to distinguish between past and present ones but if the your division is active you'll realize that different situations require different responses.

4. The Swish Method

It is one of the NLP methods that enhance the extremely restricting effects of negative thoughts. The goal of the Swish technique is to discern emotions that are passionate and mental triggers for negativity and to replace the negative thoughts with a perfect response. If you are using the Swish method it is not necessary to take any action but be aware of your options and allow your brain to trigger the "more positive state" whenever negative thoughts and feelings begin to overtake you.

Step-by-step instructions on how for implementing in the Swish Method enthusiastically:

Find the trigger for anxiety. Consider a scenario where you are nervous about the test's execution even though you've put in a lot of effort to be prepared for it. In this case the main trigger is anxiety and a sense of unease.

Next, consider the way your body and mind react to these emotions (for instance, nail gnawing, belly aches or stomach, etc.) Draw a picture of the situation in which this happens (for example , walking into the exam room).

Consider how you might idealistically want to be reacted to when you step into the space where negative thoughts occur (for instance, being certain, prepared, idealistic or even a smug, euphoric.).

This is called the suspected substitution. In your mind, visualize the negative situation and symbolically put the change in the context you've contemplated, making sure that it is more grounded, and active, while also creating the negative sensation to appear in stark contrast or unclear.

Similar to other NLP systems it is necessary to practice how to use the Swish Method a couple of times to ensure that the substitute thought is transformed into an automatic reaction. You should do it several times and increase the speed of your visualization with each round. To test for validity you must invoke the trigger thought or feeling and the specific circumstances and observe the way you feel in response to it.

It is believed that the Swish Method is a representation method based on the notion that the truth is more believable than fiction. The results of research have proven that the mind does not differentiate between real and imaginary events because both of them are able to activate similar parts in the brain. Numerous studies have shown that the type of mental exercise that is associated with representation is directly affecting fundamental abilities in the subjective, like memory, thinking and discernment. The benefits of mastering this method include improved enthusiasm execution as well as a peaceful and specific method of learning that you do not have to allow negative thoughts to dominate your life.

Chapter 2: Making-Up Of A Manipulator

Psychological manipulation involves the manipulation of people's emotions and weaknesses. The majority of people are able to defend themselves against physical attacks, however manipulators attack their targets with emotionally and psychological weaknesses.

Human beings have more vulnerability than they would like to admit, but we also have ways of protecting ourselves. Self-protection can be accomplished through developing positive mental attitudes and healthy boundaries, as well as perseverance, resilience, solid character, and the ability to defend our rights. However, these defenses naturally are weakened when we surround ourselves with people that we feel will have our best interests at heart. If we're going through a challenging time such like a divorce or illness, losing a job or loss of loved one, we're more vulnerable and vulnerable to being manipulated. This is one of the key elements of manipulative success - identifying an area of weakness or a moment that is vulnerable in the victim, and then taking advantage of it.

Manipulation is the art of Manipulation Dictionary definition of manipulation Manipulation dictionary definition

"the act of manipulating or manipulating something in a clever way'.

The act of manipulating another with a clever or untrustworthy manner'.

In these definitions of the dictionary We can see that the most important aspects are the words'skillful' and "clever". These terms highlight that Manipulation requires a certain amount of skill and intelligence. The term "unscrupulous" refers towards the idea that this is illegal or deceitful.

That's how we usually perceive Manipulation as something that is harmful, negative or undesirable. But what if you were able to discover how you can use it to live a more fulfilling life? Increase your income? Attract your dream partner? Sure, it shouldn't appear as if it were a crime?

My perception of Manipulation is that it's a subliminal method to get our desired outcomes from people willingly, even though it's not something they would typically agree to.

Nobody wants to feel like they've been made to feel like they've been a victim, but we all do play games with each other. However we find it acceptable to be controlled in certain circumstances like by salespeople or politicians for example. We might not be able to openly confess it, but we are aware that we have been manipulated. However, due to the evolution of technology, we tend to look for the positive in people. We tell ourselves that 'of course, people are in our best interest in their hearts' "of course, this salesperson would like us to buy this car as it's the right option for us, not because there's an annual sales target to meet'.

Many of us are quick to blame those who employ persuasion techniques to gain what they want, and call them manipulators. We learn about politicians who make promises to people about something to win their vote, only to change their minds once they're in charge and nothing is ever discussed about it. They don't get the same kind of backlash in the way they conduct themselves to achieve their goals as Joe Bloggs ' office.

I bring this up not to show that manipulation happens more often than we wish to acknowledge, but because mastering these skills will make us more effective communicators and teach us to guard ourselves from being manipulative.

Skilled Manipulators

Manipulators vary in their skill as well as the techniques they employ. However, what they share is the ability to get inside the mind of other people.

Highly skilled manipulators know how to identify psychological weaknesses, or the hidden desires of those they seek to are targeting However, they are also adept at using these knowledge points to entice people into action in order they can achieve something.

This art form is adept at playing with people's emotions and weaknesses in a manner that they are unable to comprehend the situation until it's late. People who manipulate develop a certain mindset that, when they find themselves in any new environment, either professionally or socially they immediately begin evaluating individuals on their worth in terms of usability, value, and vulnerability. If a suitable person has been recognized the manipulator begins analysing their facial expressions, body language behavior, mannerisms, vocabulary, and any other subtle indicators that result in an evaluation of the character and personality of the person. Once they've narrowed down the people they want to target the manipulator will work towards establishing the foundation for a closer relationship. They examine the victims to are aware of what drives them and when they feel their victim is confident enough to take their advice, take on the full-on approach.

The main goal is to be likable as well as trustworthy and welcoming typically by displaying the highest degree of understanding and empathy. If we show an curiosity in others and their interests, it will naturally weaken the defenses of those around them.

Kin Hubbard explains this stage extremely well: 'The person who is in agreement with all you declare can be either fool, or is preparing to slay you'.

Exploiting Others' Vulnerabilities

We all feel vulnerable due to any one of a number of reasons, including a deficiency of resources, in terms of social standing, physical handicaps and language barriers, and more. When working it is possible to feel at risk if we're young, less skilled or less educated than the rest of the population. In social settings there is a risk of being judged because of their status in the economy, family history or education. When it comes to relationships with other people it is possible to be at risk if they are from different backgrounds or cultures or suffer from physical disabilities or having a different sexual or religious inclination. In some societies the women who have not been divorced or married are at risk.

The primary distinction between manipulators who are skilled and more violent methods like brainwashing blackmailing, bribery, or racketeering, is that the manipulators are more gentle and do not openly attack their victims with violent threats or demands that are excessive. This is why they are extremely deadly. It's easy to defend yourself in the event that you know who the adversary is

However, in the case of manipulative behavior, the culprit typically is a trusted acquaintance or someone who you thought you could be able to trust. This can make it easier for the person being manipulated into a falsehood.

People are prone to attract manipulators, acting like a magnet. They are typically naive and nervous or unsecure people. This is not meant to criticize them however, with them the use of flattery, guilt or shame games usually result in quick outcomes.

Basic Manipulative Behaviours

1 - Use the power of your Words against you

It is a technique that is commonly employed by the majority of people and not only manipulators. It's also a efficient sales method. When we ask the most pertinent questions, we get a valuable piece of information that can be utilized against them later on at the time of. If it's an agreement to sell the salesperson might have identified your actual motivation behind buying a product, which might be the reason you want to buy a new car in order that you can visit your family during weekends. When the salesperson has uncovered the real reason behind your purchase and is able to smash you to death by threatening you to agree to the deal. It isn't easy to argue that something is proven to be true. This is the reason arguments are best won by using arguments that people make against them. You could use the phrase "you've said that' .....', or "you have done the following ...', by repeatedly highlighting another person's behavior or words that prevent the other person from challenging our arguments.

2. Refuse to accept responsibility

Manipulators could spin and deceive whenever they feel it is appropriate to avoid disagreements or disputes. Their skill is in the degree of conviction that they use to create these falsehoods. They lie in a way that makes you actually believe what they're telling.

3 3 Blame

They will try to avoid being accountable for a mistake. Instead, they'll try at shifting the blame to the weaker or vulnerable person. They'll use the victimization strategy to make others feel guilt-ridden. If they're trying to gain some benefit from your help, they might attempt to convince you to feel empathy for their struggles in order to justify your motives for aiding or helping them.

It is much easier to manipulate people certain people than other. The most successful manipulators don't always feel sorry for the hurt they could be inflicting on their victims. Their biggest advantage, which is typically an abundance of empathy, can also be their most powerful weapon.

4. Emotional Detachment

Detachment from emotion can be an extremely desirable ability for manipulators. It can be a result of emotional trauma that occurs in childhood. It is commonly referred to as emotional numbing, dissociation , or emotional blunting. It's considered unhealthy since it represents completely disconnected from emotions. It can be a result of trauma in childhood to help the child to avoid feeling hurt or painful emotions. However, when youngsters become adults they typically carry their childhood trauma with their children.

The people who are naturally manipulative likely have experienced this kind of trauma that has led to a reduction in their emotions and emotions.

Basic Manipulation Techniques

We all play tricks on other people at times, but the majority of them are harmless. The majority of them fall into the category of basic manipulation skills. A skilled manipulator would employ more sophisticated methods to hide their influence. We often employ techniques that are not as sophisticated within our everyday lives to make sure our wants are satisfied. The majority of the time, we aren't aware that we're manipulating.

There are a variety of ways that people can be forced or coerced into doing something they do not want to do The most popular techniques include guilt-tripping, complaining, lying, denying, pretending ignorance or innocence, blame the other party, using bribery, psychological blackmail or evasiveness apology, flattery, gifts, and favours As you can see, there's a lot to choose from. If we're honest the majority of us have employed a number of these tactics at least once. This doesn't mean we're sinister or evil but rather to show how widespread these techniques are.

Such as, "After everything I've done for your ...', or If your parents ever found that out ...', as well as 'There's not person in the office who can do this just like the person you ....', is just a few of the most frequently used phrases that are used to make one feel guilty or forced to comply with the request.

In this article, we will look at the fundamental strategies that are simple to master and implement.

Basic influential Techniques

Incorporate your ideas into the heads of someone else

Create a relaxed atmosphere within your workplace. People can be easily influenced if they're in an Alpha state of mind. having a calm and calm attitude helps to achieve this state.

Paying close at your words and tone, you can entice people into a state of relaxation more quickly. Check if your words and tone have the desired effect on your target's physiology the body, posture and posture. Do this with your close family members and acquaintances, observe the way they relax or get excited depending on the way you speak to them. Speak loudly or fast naturally helps people become more alert, while speaking slow and calmly is more likely to create a relaxed impact. Pay attention to the eyes. We typically see the first signs of relaxation, because pupils naturally increase in size and dilate.

You can pay close at the neck and see whether the pulse of the neck is very fast or slow. It is a process that requires practice however it could also assist in determining how the opposing person is experiencing.

The way we breathe can vary depending on the mental state of the individual. When we're at peace, we are more likely to breathe deeply , also known as 'belly breathing' however when we are stressed or stressed, breathing patterns tend to be more shallow.

If you can make people to feel at ease (large pupils) or at peace (breathing slow and deep) and comfortable within your presence (open and relaxed body position)

It's when they'll be the most vulnerable for your influence.

Use hot words

"Hot words" effectively bring emotion in the people. They are often employed in the fields of politics and sales, but they can be effective in conversations in everyday life to persuade or influence.

They may appear ordinary initially however, they're actually extremely in awe due to their connection to the senses. Words like - hear this, feel this think about it, feel comfortable, and so on. The power of these words is that they instantly trigger an emotional state through the psychological short-circuiting.

If you listen to someone carefully listen to them carefully, you can determine which words that are hot and be the most impactful for their lives. For example, if a person often says phrases like "I am not sure what the issue lies" or "I do not understand the point of it." ...". Visual learners' mental process is based upon what they are able to imagine (see). It is best to reach out to visual learners by using phrases like "See it this way" ..."," or "Look at the subject from a different perspective".

However it is a sign of disrespect when someone says something in a manner such as, "I feel they were wrong" ..."", or "I find myself lost". These people are kinesthetic learners. They are able to comprehend things through the senses. For these learners, you can make use of phrases like "I think it's what I think you need to do" or "Feel at ease to contact me at any time ...".

The second most popular kind of learning is the auditory. Be aware of those who use words like "I enjoy the sounds of this" as well as "listen to your heart".

This is simply adjusting your language and your communication to fit the way other people interpret the world. That means that your message is most likely to get noticed the way you meant to be received.

However, regardless of the personality type Certain words hold more influence over others. Journalists and salesmen are skilled at communicating and are able to make use of the appropriate words at the right moment for example, the word "cash has more power than "money, beating'. It is also more powerful than the word 'assaulted and'starving can be more effective than the word 'hungry and so on.

Humans are naturally able to switch through information that doesn't at first interest them. The words that make us feel that trigger emotions, and generate similar images and thoughts within the brain. If they are used with care they can influence the decisions of a person without needing to say anything. Through studying your target and their needs, you can learn the right words to use and how to receive the desired response.

8 fundamental steps to develop manipulative abilities

Learn to understand people. Make assumptions about people and see whether you're right.

Look nice. Always make sure you look neat, well-groomed and clean.

Use pleasant manners. Be courteous and helpful. Be courteous, friendly, and considerate.

Make yourself appear as if you are friendly, or at a minimum try to appear at least a bit friendly.

Show concern, love and empathy, offer an ear for crying.

Stay organized. When you plan a strategy for manipulation either benign or difficult it is necessary to plan your strategy From A-Z, and sometimes even altering strategies.

Develop patience. Sometimes, things don't happen as planned.

Additional qualities: ruthlessness, cunningness, emotional detachment, shrewdness.

The art of manipulation entails two major aspects: hiding your true intentions, and knowing the weaknesses of your person you are targeting.

Chapter 3: Who uses Dark Psychology?

Many people are able to employ dark psychology to benefit themselves. It is often thought that it's something we'll encounter on a regular basis and is not very common or even so significant. We are satisfied that we can remain as far from it as we can, because we believe we'll be able to identify it before it is a part of our life.

Based on the concepts we spoke about in the last chapter, it's possible to conclude that anyone could use dark psychology to achieve their desired results from others. This could be any person who is out there, so that they're safe, and are not doing any sort of harm to the people they want or to achieve their goals.

The majority of us think that we'll not be able to do harm to the people in our vicinity. We are afraid that we'll be kicked out of society and we could be in prison or some other thing would occur to us. In most cases, the fear of feeling guilt and regret as a result will be enough to keep the majority of people from engaging in the practice of dark psychology as well as various other techniques we'll cover in this article.

Everyone has some dark psychological aspects that we all have. Some of us will be able to keep it more loud than others. Some of us will be throughout our lives and be able to resist any impulse that we may have in relation to the actions and thoughts you might be tempted to take. Our ethics, laws, and more , will keep us from taking action on this, and we'll accept them and not cause harm to other people.

Some of them that have these tendencies and typically are able to maintain control. They aren't always seeking targets in the hopes of inflicting trouble on someone else. However, there could be an occasion when they cause an injury to another or maybe they witness someone else being hurt and do not feel any guilt in the least.

Maybe they are at peace and content when they do it, particularly in the event that it allowed them to achieve what they desire. They are able to ward off these dark thoughts in the majority of cases.

There will also be people who are not able to control their dark impulses or lack the desire or solution to eliminate the urges. They may believe that people are foolish because they don't take all the advantage they can to achieve what they desire. They don't have a problem with others or other things so they can help them obtain what they want.

Most of the time, pushing them to obtain what they want can harm the other person. It is not the objective that these manipulators have. They might do their best to accomplish their objective. If someone is able to be used but isn't injured in the process, then it's okay. But, if someone has to inflict harm on themselves to achieve their objectives, the dark manipulator shouldn't be feeling guilty also. That means that they do not have to inflict harm on other people in order to be a good person, however, should someone be hurt the person is.

It is likely that a lot of people be in these categories, but it doesn't mean that they work in one kind of business for one position or the other. They may have any economic or social background and may have lots of friends, or none. There isn't necessarily an individual group of people who tend to be more inclined to bend to one way or the other and it can be difficult to identify who may be in a dark place and who is capable of concealing certain impulses they feel.

However, this is a great thing for you. This means you'll be able to make use of dark psychology regardless of the background or where you are from. Some of the most powerful dark manipulators are the ones who didn't anticipate to be this, or who , at the very least, others did not think they were. This lets them join the group they wish to join and communicate to their goals without adding doubt in the process.

Dark psychology can be found within each one of us however, most of us are afraid to share it and discover where it could bring us. This is an awful thing. Because of an ethical background and so on, we are able to lose the things we'd like to to achieve in our lives and the place we'd like to be.

This doesn't mean we must be able to cause as much hurt and suffering to other people as we can but rather, it's the belief that in some instances, taking proper care of yourself and achieving your goals is the most important thingto do, instead of worrying about the morals and values of people around us. Knowing what is the most just in this regard. This guide will teach you the various ways you can apply each technique of dark psychology to be prepared to employ it when you're correct.

After we've spent an hour discussing how we can all make use of some form of dark psychology at one time or another to assist us reach the desired outcomes and reach our objectives, let's look at certain groups of people who are more likely to employ these methods and who can easily apply dark psychology into their interactions with others.

But, you might be amazed by how many people in your life employ the dark side to their advantage and could have already used you to achieve their advantage. A few of the people that could benefit from dark psychology are:

1. Narcissists: Individuals who fulfill the diagnostic criteria of being narcissists will see their self-esteem elevated. They must have other people around to prove that they are more superior. They believe that other people will love and admire them. If they have to manipulate, use impure persuasion, dark psychology and so on then they will.

2. Sociopaths: true sociopaths are charming and intelligent however, they can also be extremely impulsive. Because of their lack of emotionality and the inability to not feel guilt, sociopaths may employ tricks to create an appearance of a relationship and, thus, benefiting the person they are attempting to benefit.

3. Attorneys: A few lawyers concentrate so much on winning the case that they'll use obscure methods of persuasion, as well as other strategies to ensure they obtain the desired result.

4. Politicians: there are a lot of occasions when politicians employ these strategies to convince people that they're right and aid in gaining votes.

5. Sellers: Some sellers may not be as ethical as they ought to be and will try to make the sale by negotiating

With the help of some dubious tactics. They do this to convince another person, who are their clients, to purchase the product, even though they are able to monitor the customers.

6. Leaders: Some managers employ these tactics in order to ensure compliance, important effort, or better performance from those below them.

7. Public Speakers Certain speakers are willing to employ these unsavory strategies to boost the emotional level of their audience in the hope that it leads to the sales of several items in behind the scenes, and the ability to achieve what their audience is looking for to learn from.

8. Any person who is really selfish. This could be any person who has an agenda for himself ahead of other people. They'll use the strategy to satisfy their own needs first, and even at someone other's expense. They do not care if someone else is hurt during the process.

It is evident that lots of different people benefit from it, especially when using dark psychology and often use it. Although there are a variety of instances when we can use persuasion and manipulation as well as other techniques safely and safely to achieve what you desire, unscrupulous tactics ensure that the person who uses it receives the desired outcome regardless of what even if another person suffers harm. Let's look at the various things you have to know about dark psychology to realize the benefits you seek.

Chapter 4: What You Can Do to Be Safe From Manipulation

Manipulation typically occurs when one person is used for the benefit of other people. This is when the manipulator has an imbalance of power , and uses it to benefit the victim to further their own agendas. The manipulative types are those who cover up their motives and desires as yours. They will do everything they can to get you to believe that their opinions are true. They'll then behave like they're being snatched away. They will claim to provide help to improve your performance, attitude and claim to assist you in improving your overall life. This is what they would like you to believe. The truth is the main purpose of these people is to dominate you and not to control you in the way they want you to believe. They don't care about making your life better they just want to alter your life. They want to prove their lives and ensure that you do not outgrow them.

After you've reintroduced the characters back to your life eliminating them isn't an easy task. They can appear to switch between matters and appear to be a bit sloppy when you are trying to be accountable to them. They can also make promises to assistance that doesn't appear to be on the horizon.

People are susceptible to being manipulated by those who choose to tolerate passive aggressive behaviours. According to a report published in The Journal of Social & Personal Relationships the most offensive people are likely to hinder the general performance of an individual. The study also revealed that not ignoring people who are negative may cause your body more damage than positive. When people are ignored it is proven that their intelligence and productivity are raised. More than 100 participants were studied to conduct this study. Participants were instructed to avoid or converse with anyone that are either rude or friendly.

Participants were unaware about the kind of people they would have to meet. After about 4 minutes, each participant was given the opportunity to think about a problem that required them to work at a higher level of concentration. The research later revealed that those who did not pay attention to the criminals performed more effectively than the ones who employed with them.

The researchers concluded the fact that keeping a distance from certain individuals when they are engaged in intense social interactions is an effective way to protect a person's psychological resources. The best approach is to avoid people who have negative attitudes in their actions and words. However, sometimes, that isn't enough. Someone who is cynical may be devious and sneaky at times. In such instances you'll try to employ other methods.

Being manipulative isn't a great way to live. The only thing that could be worse that manipulation is confessing our dark secrets. When we discover that we've been manipulated by someone else, we feel embarrassed and humiliated and weak. Then it doesn't stop there. When we fall prey to the lies that these people play on us, they'll leave us with a terrible feeling about the world surrounding us. Instead of getting hurt yet another occasion, the most effective option could be to not trust anyone.

Manipulation will only succeed If the person being targeted fails to acknowledge it or decide to let it happen. However, regardless of that, there are certain actions you can take to realize that you're in the midst of manipulative power. They could also help to avoid or stop any potential manipulation. Certain ideas might not be appropriate or feasible in your particular situation However, that's okay because every situation and person is different.

Be aware of your rights fundamentals

One of the most important guidelines to follow when you're in this kind of situation is to understand the fundamental rights you have. However, it's not the only thing to do. You must also be aware the violation of one of these rights. Be aware that you are free to speak in your own defense and make sure there is that there is no violation of your fundamental rights. But, it is important to be careful and make sure you don't cause harm to other people. Don't ignore the possibility of losing the rights you have if you cause injury to another person. Be sure to be aware of certain fundamental rights of the human being, such as:

The right
being treated with respect and respect.

To voice one's desires thoughts, opinions, and desires.

Give no answer and continue to do so without guilt.

In order to establish your standards and priorities.

Be careful and protect yourself from being mentally, emotionally or physically attacked.

The rights mentioned above show how far your boundaries ought to extend. We live in a world that doesn't recognize the rights of any of these. The psychological manipulators are particularly attracted to denying you your rights, so they are able to completely manage you and profit of your rights. But, you hold the legal authority, morality and authority to assert that you're in control of your life and not the one who manipulates you.

Keep a safe distance from these individuals

As mentioned, one of the most reliable methods of identifying an individual who is manipulative is to see whether the person is acting in a different manner when the presence of different people and situations. Although we all are adept at this technique of social differentiation, mental manipulators are experts in their ability to live in extremes, where they display great humility towards one person, and are be rude to another. They may also appear angry at one time and then helpless in the next. If you observe this type of behavior among those you're close to The best thing to do is maintain a healthy distance. Try to stay clear of those who are exhibiting this behavior until you feel forced to do so. Be aware that the most common causes of psychological manipulation are deeply rooted and intricate, so helping or changing the behavior of these people is not your responsibility.

Stop Self-Blaming and Personalization

If the manipulator is able to discover what your weaknesses are and then exploit the weakness, you might blame you for not being a good enough person. It is crucial to assure yourself that you're not a part of the problem when you are in such a situation. Keep in mind that you're being controlled to feel guilty for your actions, and then surrender your rights and powers at the final. It is crucial to take into consideration the type relationships you share with your manipulator, as well. These are just a few questions you need to consider asking yourself:

Am I getting respectful treatment?

Is this relationship one-way or two-way?

Do I feel content being with this person?

The solutions to these questions will provide the most significant clues as to the issue, whether it is the person who is manipulating you or.

Check the Manipulators

Mental manipulators always make demands or demands of you. They will do this in order to get you to push yourself to the limit to meet their demands. In some instances, it could be necessary to concentrate on the manipulator every when you are contacted with specific requests. You can ask them some of the questions to determine if they're completely aware of their plan's unfairness. Find out if their actions seem reasonable to them, or if what they're seeking from you is fair.

If you decide to ask these questions, you're just putting up a mirror so the person manipulating you will be aware of the motive behind his or her strategy. If the manipulator turns out to be an expert in self-awareness, then they will retreat and then regress. However, true pathological manipulators will ignore the issue and insist on going about their own way. When this happens be sure to protect your fundamental rights so that the manipulators leave.

Say No in a firm and diplomatic Way

Refusing to accept a refusal is a clear and diplomatic approach to what is considered to be genuine communication. It lets you be firm and ensure the most productive relation after a sufficient amount of articulation. It is essential to remember the fact that among your most fundamental rights as a human being is the right to establish your standards and your priorities. You also have the right to refuse without guilt, and the freedom to decide on your own happy and healthy life.

Determine the consequences

If a mind-controlled person continues in breaking the boundaries you set and does not hear the "no," you will be forced to take the consequences. Being able to clearly identify and defend the goods is among the key abilities you have to use to thwart a manipulative individual's efforts. When these are clearly communicated results can stop the manipulative individual's actions, and may even force them to end the infringements and to show respect instead.

Face your Bullies in a secure Way

The one thing that's not well known for many people is the fact that a psychological manipulator could become the role of a bully when they attempt to intimidate and hurt other people. It is crucial to remember that bullies will only target those they believe to be the weakest. You are a potential victim if you are apathetic and oblivious. The reality is that the majority of bullies are cowards on their inside. They often retreat when their victim starts to assert their rights. This is an everyday procedure in offices and in their surroundings as well as at schoolyards.

Think about the long-term implications of your choices

Instead of taking the option that is the most convenient and speediest Do not forget the consequences of your actions. Keep in mind that psychological manipulators are the best in making their choices the most pleasant, the most swift, and most non-harmful. They also excel at keeping focus on the present feelings. This is why people make decisions they later regret later. Instead of enduring consequences later ensure that you decide to make a decision that you aren't forced to reconsider.

Chapter 5: The Different Types Of Manipulation

Cognitive

There are many well-known psychological processes that are part of theories about the art of manipulating. One of these are the cognitive response model invented in 1968 by Anthony Greenwald in 1968. It's still in use today to determine the factors that contribute to persuasion. It is also that is widely utilized in the world of advertising.

Greenwald suggested:

It's not the language or message itself that determine the efficacy of manipulation rather the emotions of the person receiving it. The inner monologue of person who is who is receiving the message will determine the degree to which they are affected.

These thoughts in the mind will have positive and negative components depending on the person's personal characteristics. This is not a learning process and is more dependent on the fact that the individual already perceives the message in a positive or unfavorable thoughts (cognitions).

Reciprocity

Another reason that has been studied for why we could be susceptible to manipulative power is the Rule of Reciprocity. This is based upon an idea that is connected to social norms. If you are a victim of a kindness or is kind to you, you are more likely to feel obligated to repay the favor.

This Rule of Reciprocity can also be a result of a subconscious decision. While you aren't aware of it you might accept a decision, or request a favor from the person asking for it.

At the time, they done something for you and you are that you owe them. You might feel obliged, even when the request is one you normally would not accept.

It is a technique widely employed by companies seeking to generate sales. Many companies offer free samples or trial periods. It is not without motive. It hopes that the client feels obligated to repay the favor and purchase the item or keep the contract in place.

Reciprocity is a well-known psychological phenomenon. It's an adaptive behaviour which could have enhanced the chances to survive in past times. When you assist others, it is possible that, in the future they will assist you.

But, it could also cause negative consequences. If someone has done something wrong towards you, you could be compelled by the rules of reciprocity to get your revenge.

Information Manipulation

This is a potent weapon in the armory of the manipulator. It is a technique of deceitful and openly lying. It's a way of providing only a small amount of details on the subject. The result is that it will cause them to think differently and make them more vulnerable. This can also include the use of deliberate body language in order to convince and influence someone.

A study conducted by McCornack and co. (1992) demonstrated the many ways in which a message may be falsified in manipulating the process. McCornack's theory is founded on the premise of four principles that form the truthfulness of a assertion. If you violate any of these could render the statement to be fraudulent. The four principles are:

Quantity

The term refers to what we call the "amount" amount of data given. We all want to give the correct amount of information that the recipient can comprehend the message. It's not too little, nor excessively, since it could cause confusion. A manipulator could play with the quantity of data. They might omit some pieces they believe are irrelevant, particularly in the event that they will oppose their arguments. This is referred to as "lying by the omission."

Quality

The term refers on what is the "accuracy" in the data given. A truthful communication is one that is high quality. If we violate this principle and the receiver is notified, they hear deliberately false information. It's "outright being deceived" to enhance the manipulation's power.

Relationship

In this article, we discuss what we call the "relevance" of this information in relation to the message. To confuse or avoid an awkward situation the manipulator could wander off-topic. This is a means to alter the subject with the sole reason of deceiving. This could be done to conceal their flaws. It could also be to exaggerate something to give the speaker more control over their audience.

Manner

The latter is an important aspect of the "presentation" of the information. A key aspect to this process is the body language. We are able to read facial expressions when we listen. A manipulator might overstate these in order to deceive the way they present their message. All of this is in the effort to highlight their goals.

Persuading or manipulating an individual isn't an entirely new idea. It is an approach that is becoming more effective in the present day. Social media and online communication are not all about face-to-face contact. This makes it much easier to lie or embellish facts. A manipulator could be working in their element by using these communications.

Nudge

There are no sinister methods of manipulation. Sometimes, we are manipulated to assist us in making the right choices to benefit us. For this it is recommended that it is suggested that the Nudge Theory is particularly useful. Nudge

Theory Nudge Theory expands positive reinforcement with small Nudges.

Skinner's behaviorism studies show how effective this theory can be. Positive reinforcement, for example, rewards, can entice individuals into acting in the way you wish to influence.

One instance of "nudging" can be observed in this instance. Incorporating items with high prices on a menu could appear unproductive. But, the outcome is that it increased sales of the second-highest priced item. The customers were offered an "nudge" to move in the proper direction, but only for the benefit of the restaurant owner.

Richard Thaler, considered the Nudge Theory father, was given with the Nobel Memorial Prize in Economic Sciences. The contribution he made to behavioral economics was regarded as significant. Nudge Theory gives positive reinforcement or, as Thaler stated the theory gives "nudges."

It is important to note that the Nudge Theory is not only efficient in the field of economics. It can also be employed to motivate behavioral changes and influence choices made by individuals. Even social norms that are accepted by the majority of people are manipulated to change in this manner.

Nudging is so effective that in 2010 the British Government created the Department Behavioral Insights Team. It was created to assist in developing policies. The department was known in the form of the Nudge Unit.

There are obvious advantages of making use of "nudges" for influencing individuals. However, it is still a method of psychological manipulation that could violate a person's rights to privacy.

Social Manipulation

This kind manipulative technique is referred to as psychological manipulative. It is usually a tool for the political class or other powerful groups of people that are employed to advance their own goals. In its worst case it's a tool to control the social order. Through the elimination of individuality it forces people to accept what is presented to them. However, it could be beneficial in helping with personal issues, like improving health and well-being.

The people in power who employ social manipulation could employ distractive methods to distract from crucial issues. They may claim that their plans serve the interests of the population and the benefit of your family as well as its future. Anything that you feel personally could be different from the norm is untrue and selfish. This kind of persuasion is extremely paternalistic, treating people as if they are all kids. This "system" is designed to convince the masses that the things that went wrong are, in reality they are their own fault. Only way to solve the issue is to follow the advice of those who are more knowledgeable.

A political strategy like this would expose one social issue, but then to conceal another. It's a tactic that aims to create social tension and anxiety among the population. Through creating a sense of unease within society, people will be compelled to make changes. For instance, the department wants to conceal the issues with health care. Therefore, they reduce the budget for prevention of crime, which causes the crime rate to increase. The public will be provided with information that will force them to believe in the most effective solution to the problem of crime. Politicians will spread propaganda by disseminating personal truths and figures. It might not be accurate or may contain inaccurate like the use of statistics in a way that is not true. This kind of manipulation can take years to reach the desired result that the person who is manipulating wants.

Psychological manipulations are an aspect of social influence. Prof. Preston Ni,

Communication Studies released an article on Psychology Today. He states that one group is aware of the weaknesses of the other. They are determined to create a conflict of power. This allows them to profit from their victims to further their motives.

Do we all become social puppets? In some ways it certainly does. We all comply and adhere to the expectations of others to keep from a world of chaos.

Consider for a moment, what is the most recent device or home improvement item that you'd like to purchase? Are you looking for something that a family member said they had or that a neighbor has? Most likely, it's something you've seen someone else own or you've read that it's well-known online, which is what makes you want it. Another aspect of manipulation through social media. We are easily influenced when we don't keep our guards up. If that's a good or bad thing will depend on the way you view it.

It is not all manipulation of social networks an issue. It has positive sides. The term "manipulation" could bring up images of villains who manipulate your will. However, when used properly manipulating social networks can benefit the general population. One of the best examples of manipulation in social media include the "5 days a week" campaigns." Health experts try to persuade that we eat more fruits and vegetables. Even the "stop smoking campaign," which have resulted in a decrease in smokers. This results in reduced incidence of smoking-related illnesses. This is coercion at its finest.

Gaslighting

It is possibly the most brutal method of manipulative behaviour. It's a way to question the credibility and self-esteem of an individual. It could be described as planting doubt seeds to the person who is being manipulated. Based on the same principle like "knowing you're constantly being told lies." Then, eventually, you come to accept the lies as the truth.

It's a cruel form of manipulative behavior. The gas-lighter can cause the victim to lose faith in their own self-worth. This will cause them to lose their self-esteem. The reason for this is that they begin to doubt their own worth. That's the goal of gaslighting in order to cause the victim to become an emotional mess. The manipulator is always trying to bring their target down by denying their claims. They will also convince them that they're always right. Sometimes, to the point where the victim is accused of lying. The victim's self-esteem is destroyed. If this happens the victim is subjugated by the dominant influencer. This is a type of mental abuse that is often found in abusive relationships. The person who is in control will employ constantly to cause their victim to doubt. To the point of being unable to remember certain things they've done or said.

It can take a few minutes before it can be completely efficient. The manipulator wears his or her victim down over a lengthy time. This kind of manipulation is so devious that it may cause the victim to doubt their credibility.

The Dr. George Simon PhD is a Clinical Psychologist working at the Texas university. He has examined people who have troublesome personality traits. The results of his research led him to conclude that certain kinds of individuals, such as psychopaths, are extremely skilled in manipulating. They can distort the truth and use a violent language to set wheels of doubt within their victims' minds. In the end, the victim will doubt their judgement. They may be embarrassed and will begin believing that their manipulator has the right. This puts the victim in the hands of the manipulator.

Gaslighting isn't just limited to those who act on the other. It could be said that it has also the potential to be used for political purposes. Author and columnist Maureen Dowd is one to adhere to this view. She claimed that the Clinton administration employed gaslighting techniques to sway opposition politicians. Newt Gingrich, a candidate of the opposition political party was often manipulated to appear hysterical. Psychologists and journalists have argued the fact that Donald Trump also used gas-lighting methods. Not just in his campaign for president,, but even while in office. People argue that he often says something, and later denies he did it this is known as gas-lighting.

Chapter 6: What is Influence and Persuasion?

There are many instances where humans are easily influenced, but it takes certain skills to convince people to sit down and pay attention to your message. Not all people are adept at influence and persuasion. They could talk for hours and still be unable to persuade others to follow their own ideas. However there are those who can convince anyone to do whatever they would like, even if they'd just met the individual for the very first time. Learning how to use these abilities can help you to identify the signs of a manipulator and be in avoiding the person if they are needed.

The first thing is worth examining is the definition of persuasion. Persuasion is the method or act taken by a particular person or group of people who are looking to influence something to change. It could be in relation to another person or things that alter their internal mental structures or in their behavior patterns on the outside.

Persuasion when performed correctly, can result in something completely new for the person, or could simply alter something that is that is already in their mind. Three distinct parts are involved in this process, including:

* The communicator or another source of persuasion

It is persuasive.

* The audience or person who is the target of the appeal

The three factors mentioned above should be considered prior to attempting any type of persuasion of your own. It is easy to look at the people living in your life and you'll see a variety of kinds of persuasion taking place everywhere.

These are all positive ways you can make use of persuasive techniques for your benefit. The majority of people will be open to these methods. However, on the flip side you can use four negative methods of persuasion that you may use as well. This includes options such as manipulating, avoidance or intimidating others, and even threat. These tactics that are negative will be much easier for the target identify, which is the reason most manipulators would be careful to avoid them whenever possible.

Then, you can apply one or more of the strategies that we have discussed above. However, according to the psychology expert Robert Cialdini, six major concepts of persuasion will help you achieve the results you desire with the goal of not having to discern what's happening. Let's look at these 6 weapons and the ways they are effective.

The six tools of influence

Reciprocity

The method of persuasion you can apply is called reciprocity. This is based on concept that when you provide something to someone else, they'll feel grateful to you and desire to repay you. Humans are wired that way in order to survive. To make it easier for the manipulator to take this strategy, they'll ensure that they're doing some sort of favor to the person they are targeting. This could include offering them a nice gesture or giving them an Uber ride on their way to work, helping with a huge project or helping them get free of becoming a target. After the favor has been done and the person receiving the favor feels like they owe something toward the manipulator. The manipulator will be able ask for something and it will be extremely difficult for the person who is being targeted to refuse.

Consistency and commitment

Humans are prone to choose what has been previously tested and proven inside the head. We all have a preconceived notion of what we're about and what we should expect to be. The majority of people are not likely to try new things, and therefore they'll continue following the same path as they were before. To get them to adhere to this idea and to do what you wish it is first necessary to convince them to be committed to your goal. The steps you'd have to follow to convince your desired outcome to be what you want by committing and commitment include:

Begin by doing something simple. It is possible to ask the target to take a small step and easy to handle the change before they begin to integrate the habit into their daily routine and begin to become hooked on the routine.

* You can convince your target to accept the issue in public so that they feel more pressured to carry it out.

• Reward the target if they are able to stay on track. Rewards will increase the motivation of the person during the course of action you would like to see them take.

Social evidence

Another one relies on human nature, and relies upon the notion that we believe in and trust in the opinions of others and their views on things we haven't attempted before. This is especially true if you get the information from a family member or someone who is considered to be an expert. It's impossible to test every aspect of life, and relying on others could make us vulnerable. That's why we have to locate a trustworthy source to to begin. A manipulator might be able to persuade an individual to perform a task by presenting themselves as someone close to them or as an expert. They can get the subject to try an action plan because they've established themselves as the person who has the best knowledge of the issue or the course of action.

Influence is a powerful yet often ineffective tool. The power to influence or change the opinions of others or to cause an environment that is more favorable to change without imposing the change directly is an art all its own. The ability to create changes or changes that change as circumstances develop can have a lasting effects. It may cause people to look up and be aware of you and your actions and can make you appear more attractive which can make people want to be able to count on them in the near future. We will discuss the methods to influence others as well as how to develop your abilities in the influence of others, and then how to make use of the influence you've developed to accomplish your objectives.

Influence is based on fundamental and fundamental factors. It's a good idea to start by entering a room that is full of people you don't have any contact with. The way you enter this room is essential. It is possible that you don't know anybody, but the majority of people is aware of it. Being yourself with the best manner of presentation within the initial few seconds of your appearance will usually determine how everyone else in the room perceives you. Smile when you step into the room, and walk with your head and back in a straight and relaxed manner. Take your time and don't rush or walk too fast

Imagine you're walking into a space in your own home. A common trick that makes you appear more approachable is to simply give a brief gesture, as if you are acknowledging someone you have known. It makes people believe that you are addressing someone else who already knows you . This is what will make you appear more likable or intriguing.

If you are meeting for the first time looking at them and holding their hand with firmness while smiling increases your charisma with your fellow. Charisma is about what you can make another person feel present. Charisma does not mean being the center of attention at the gathering. To enhance your charisma, you must first think about your strengths. Are you funny? Are you outgoing and social? Do you find yourself timid and quieter? You can make use of those strengths for your benefit, it's all about knowing how to make use of your strengths to benefit yourself. If you're more of an introvert, choose just a couple of people from the crowd or in the room to interact with. If you are attempting to initiate communication, utilize your more secluded presence to let other people do the bulk of the talking. You should just direct the conversation towards the direction you wish to move it in when it is needed. People are prone to talking about themselves! If you're social or in a position that is empowering you can approach large groups of people and say hello to them. Use the strengths you have to benefit.

The people who have influence over other people can confirm, influence is all about giving and take. If people believe that the relationship is built on reciprocity, they can feel more confident in the relationship, quicker, and are less likely to have concerns. Do a little favor from someone, and then offer them the same thing in exchange. One example is offering to take someone's place on the line for them to go to the restroom, and taking notes for them as they leave for a moment during a presentation or meeting and asking for them to take the same action when they return. This kind of exchange creates an underlying foundation of friendship in the sense that you and your counterpart are already friends. It is also a sign that people who feel you are a fan of them, will adore them in return.

It's not straightforward, but it could be done by being and being friendly. Smiles and eye contact can affect the way you make others feel. If you show that you're content to be around people who are content to speak with them, they'll also feel content to have a conversation with you. Your body language is a powerful indicator and others notice the message you're sending through your body language even though they're not completely aware of it. When you are talking to someone else be aware of the way they're standing or sitting. If they're sitting with their arms by their sides, try to imitate their posture. Imitating the body language of someone else is another method of establishing an unspoken yet solid base. If they're clearly showing tension, try mimicking their posture. A good example could be when they have their arms crossed over to the side of their bodies in a defensive position. After a couple of minutes of conversation, you can move your arms into more relaxed and natural posture. In the majority of cases those you're talking to will be able to subconsciously shift their body language to match your personal style. This is a good illustration of how you're already building trust and influence with someone that you do not have any contact with.

If you are talking to people who you would like to influence over, a second aspect to take into consideration is your personal attitudes towards them. It is well-known that your body language plays a part, and the reciprocation is also important however equally important is the way you present your image of yourself. A smile when greeting someone is excellent, but after the conversation is in progress you should maintain a neutral and relaxed face. Engaging and paying attention to the conversation will make them feel comfortable speaking with you. Making sure you ask questions according to the flow of conversation proves that you're paying attention to them. Everyone is looking to feel heard. Being calm, respectful and professional when you interact makes you more approachable and friendly. Thanking them for their time and appreciation will inspire others to appreciate your time and attention in the future.

Chapter 7: A Comprehensive Study of Manipulation

When we speak of manipulative methods that don't require using force or influencing an individual's finances, we're speaking about manipulation that is psychological in nature. Psychological manipulation is one type of influence on society that is accomplished through deceitful or hidden methods, alters a person's views of reality and their behaviour.

Manipulation is further divided into two types which are negative and positive manipulation. Positive manipulation happens when someone is manipulating for their own benefit. A good example could be an acupuncturist trying to convince a patient to quit smoking. Negative manipulation, on the other hand, involves manipulating someone else for reasons other than personal gain or for ulterior motives. A case of negative manipulation is an agent who convinces a client to purchase a product that is known to be defective or not appropriate for the purchaser.

George Simon posits that manipulation is basically a matter of two things, the first being the ability to cover up anger or other negative motives as well as the ability to detect people. People who manipulate need to identify the weaknesses of the people they wish to manipulate to gain advantage in order to gain advantage. They also need to be highly skilled in understanding the motivations of people and how they behave.

The year 1996 was the time Simon wrote a book on self-help entitled In Sheep's Clothing Understanding and Managing Manipulative People. In the book, he asserted that successful manipulators generally:

Be aware of their victim's psychological weaknesses. For instance, a mom will do anything when she believes that the actions she takes will benefit the wellbeing to her children. In the same way, if someone has fear of crowds, it can be used to entice people into not attending the party (for instance) by saying that you anticipate large numbers of people to attend.

* Are ruthless. Manipulators should be uncompromising in order to not have moral concerns about influencing people the way they do. Not being concerned about the wellbeing of the person you're manipulating typical.

* Can cover up their emotions and use this to their advantage. This is logical, if you consider it. In an official debate at high school is an awful idea and could affect no one; however crying while trying to get an loan will definitely benefit you since you'd have to make the person feel the same way.

Simon went on to study even more to study the strategies that manipulators employ to influence others. The methods vary from deceit, innocence and confusion, to playing victim and obviously seduction.

Simon is not the only psychologist to have investigated manipulators and their strategies. Harriet Braiker was a clinical psychologist who gained notoriety in the year 2000 through her novel, The Disease to Please, in which she talked about how easily influenced by people-pleasers. In her novel of 2004 titled Who is Pulling the Strings she further developed the notion of manipulation, but this time the focus was on the manipulators. Braiker identified four distinct ways manipulators can influence their victims:

Punishment. This does not mean that punishment is the same as the way a parent punishes a child for, say by shoving them down. Manipulators employ social punishment to make sure they exert their power over other people. The most commonly used type that social punishment takes is silent treatment, which is when they exclude someone from certain events, or create an acrimony between the victim and their relatives or friends.

Positive reinforcement. Simply put it's flattery. The manipulators might try to gain their way by lavishing the person they intend to influence with praise, or even by doing them a favor (like providing them with coffee before they go to work). Positive reinforcement can be as simple as a smile, or a hug or as lavish as attracting attention to the person they wish to influence.

Negative reinforcement. Negative reinforcement even though it's a misleading term it doesn't involve punishment. It's more of a different kind of reward. A manipulator who uses negative reinforcement could declare, "You don't have to go to the meeting on Monday if you drive me to the shopping mall today." In this manner the manipulator is able to free the person they want for to influence to do something they don't wish to do by, in essence inducing them to accept the manipulator's suggestion.

Traumatic single-time learning. The manipulator has to make an impact so profound on the person wants to influence that no punishment or reinforcement is required. One example could be an eruption of anger that is so overwhelming that the person who is on the receiving end doesn't even think about disobeying.

The various ways where manipulators manipulate people share a common characteristic that is regretlessness. The most remorseless of all? The psychopath. Psychopathy can be described as a psychological illness that is characterized by a lack of compassion or remorse extreme manipulation in addition to antisocial behavior and self-esteem. They are the masters of manipulative behavior and , therefore despite their less than excellent reputation, they make great role models to follow to master the art of manipulating. Robert Hare and Paul Babiak believed that psychopaths work by manipulating their victims using the three phases of.

The first stage is known by the term assessment. In this phase, the psychopath decides on whom they want to control. They are always looking for characteristics such as the status of their client, wealth, or influence, and rarely pursue those who have nothing to offer.

The next phase is called the manipulation phase in which the psychopath meticulously develops the character that the person they intend to manipulate will be aware of. After this mask is in place the psychopath will start eliciting whatever they'd like from their extremely trusting, willing victim.

The third and final stage is known as the "abandonment" phase. Once the psychopath has gotten everything they've ever wanted from the person they've controlled then they take off the mask and leave the life of the victim. When the victim has no value to the psychopath, they is not going to see any reason to continue to have a relationship with them.

Chapter 8: Dark Persuasion Methods

Trigger strategies are frequently employed under different names and are often referred to as stimulated strategies and forced strategies. The only method to persuade that someone else to think or behave in a specific manner, and that is through persuasion. Persuasion is a way to talk to the person in question while offering evidence. To alter the thinking of an object they could use any kind that of pull or force on an object. Additionally, they could provide assistance for this issue or employ various strategies. This section outlines the various ways of stimulation that are available for each method , as well as their effectiveness.

Violence and violence

In certain situations persuaders could think it's better to resort to some kind of violence in order to address the issue. This could happen when the arguments don't work when regular conversations don't work, or if an agency is in a good position. Unhappy or regretful about the manner of communication. Violence is frequently used as a terror tactic since the subject does not have the time to think about the issue logically than they do during normal conversations. Coercion is typically employed when the persuaders have little success using other methods of coercion. But, violence is an option. You can also resort to violence when the agent is out of control or the agent has contradictions to the evidence and the agent is angry.

Utilizing violence in relation to violence is usually not the best option.

In the process of stimulation. This is due to the fact that many students perceive that violence is a danger because they have no other choice but to rely on the use of violence. The desire is to select a route towards the lesson, however when power is added to the mix it becomes difficult to make your choice. Instead of feeling afraid. If the subject appears to be intimidating, an client is less likely or consider the person. Because of this, the use of force in the field of coercion is usually not recommended and is not to be to be avoided. In contrast to other forms of mental control.

Influence weapon

Another strategy that can be employed to persuade an individual to bend in a certain manner is to make use of available weaponry that can be used to cause impact. Robert Chardini created these six influences in his famous book. Persuasion techniques have six objectives. Persuaders are able to achieve these. Six weapons of influence include reciprocity, determination and perseverance, social proof, empathy empowerment and inadequacy. It is vital to ensure that the agent has one of the six weapons that have influence.

In a Mutual Way

The most powerful weapon for influence is mutual political. The idea is that an influencer offers something to another. If the value is present it tries to provide the agent with. It is a result of this that persuaders sometimes feel required to provide an equivalent service for the agent if they provide services in relation to. While the two types of services aren't identical but they are similar.

Everyone is equally.

The experience ultimately builds the feeling of duty to the subject. It is a great instrument if the persuader wishes to trigger. Interactive rules can be very beneficial because they assist the agent to put the subject in the right mindset to be coerced. Inject the feeling of duty and let it drown. In this instance the feeling of duty is a reason to convince a person that they'll behave and behave in a particular manner.

Another benefit of persuasion is the use of interaction

Moral position that imposes obligations on objects. This is a stance that is backed by norms of society. The person who persuades does not need to think about whether there's an ethical code that will reciprocate the favor. If the recipient does not believe that this is required Persuader can use the various tools available to use them. As a group, people dislike people who don't repay or even pay for products or services. If the person who persuades doesn't believe that their classes are coming towards or away from them, they may want to involve them in the social circle of their choice.

It is possible to share this information by telling your acquaintances and friends how much you are enjoying the subject. The information is not returned if it is required. Persuader is currently advocating socialization classes, by referring to volunteers, increasing their chances of convincing people to take action.

In the majority of cases the lessons are easily given back to the agent.

There is no necessity to external strength. If the need is discovered the agent is looking for ways to pay back the agent. The score is uniform and doesn't appear unselfish or greedy. Persuaders are able to provide a simple way to pay off these debts. The lesson-learning process is a simple solution, and a persuader is more likely to follow through with what they would like to do.

Engagement and sustainability

The second weapon of influence to be discussed is sustainability and commitment. Persuaders must employ both when trying to convince people to make a change. From their perspective. If things go smoothly it is easy to comprehend and the lessons can help to improve their results. However, it doesn't alter the fact that persuaders will always make use of it, or alter any other information that needs material to process. Instead of aiding. Persuasion that is consistent renders the person appear to be an untrustworthy person, which results in the demise of the process of induction.

The most crucial elements of the process for stimulus is the persistence.

Reason:

It is essential to work hard for society. In most instances, people want things to happen in specific.

There are many different kinds of life that we experience, however, most people think that the whole thing is more constant.

They are able to remember what they did and know what to expect and be ready to adapt. If there's no consistent information, it can be very difficult to plan your activities,

It's always a confusing issue. If you are looking to be convinced in a subject it is important to ensure that the facts are relevant and consistent.

Stable

It improves the daily behavior of the majority of people. Have you ever attempted to plan an entire day only to have something unplanned occurs? It can make things impossible and can end. It can feel like a catastrophe. People appreciate patience because they know the right thing to expect and how to do.

They know when they should eat when they need to work, and when to complete other tasks.

Stability is a valuable summary of the current issues in life. It's enough to live without it.

Add those which don't. If people are able to sustain their lives it will be simpler.

Sustainability is an excellent instrument because it allows you to make the right choices and analyze data. If it is, the person is looking to convince the subject. It is important to ensure that the message is clear and uniform. There's no way for false information to come out later on and ruin the entire process. Be sure the facts are correct and true and trust that the subject is excellent.

The key to lasting is the need for engagement. It requires a dedication to ensure that the name is real and worthy of the effort. Advertising is the act of purchasing the product, while political involves voting for candidates who are specific to a product. The level of commitment is determined by the kind of trust. Based on the notion of sustainability, one could be influenced by a commitment when engaged in writing or verbally proved to be more authentic writing assignments, titles can be extremely psychologically specific and provide solid evidence of their agreement to the agreement. It is logical. Many people promise to fix, or take action however they never do. Of course, there are people who are willing to do what they promised.

It is more likely that you promise verbally than if you don't, but frequently it's difficult to get the desired outcome. Additionally there is no way to prove this, since it is only a verbal promise. there's a disagreement and nobody will prevail. However when the agent is able to verify that in writing, they will have sufficient evidence to prove that the matter is done.

It is essential that the you convince your audience to accept the requirement since they tend to behave in a manner that is in line with the obligation when a new method is adopted. The most crucial thing is that the subject is not abandoned, and you'll be able to convince yourself that this is the case. The other participants will offer numerous arguments and arguments to justify your participation to prevent issues with agents. If the agent can resolve the issue at hand then there is nothing the agent needs to do.

Social proof

It is a type of social interaction, therefore it should be governed by the social norms that apply. It is influenced by people who are around you. What they would like others to do, instead rather than doing the work themselves. Classes is a reflection of their opinions and actions, the way others around them do, the way similar people act, and what they think about. If, for instance, your subject was born in a town, you tend to behave differently than the other residents. Contrarily people who were raised in a religiously-based community

The time is now to pray, to learn and assist others.

In this regard it is believed that the expression "power of the masses" is extremely useful. Students are always interested in knowing what the other classes are doing in their vicinity. It's almost hilarious to follow the same path as others in our country. What people think about and how they would like in their lives as individuals has to be agreed upon.

The actions of people are recorded on the phone as others have been doing things. Host "Waiting for an operator to call; you must call me immediately." You may feel as if an operator is sitting in the middle in silence because no one is calling. This makes it harder for users to call since they shouldn't make a phone call when there's no one in the room. The host only changes one or two words and instead "If you find that the person on the line is not available, try calling another time." The results are very different. In this case, the Chancellor assumes the operator is calling multiple clients. Therefore, the system has to be efficient and systematic. The more likely the subject is be prone to phone calls, regardless of whether they have passed or are required to be suspended immediately.

Induction technology

Social evidence can be extremely beneficial when the goal is not clear, or where there are numerous similarities to the scenario. In uncertain or ambiguous situations that have a variety of choices or options, subjects typically choose to follow what others are doing. The choices are all alike, and so they are all logical, but suppose that the choices taken by other people are right. Another method to utilize social evidence is to look for similarities. For instance classes focus on certain individuals, and they are more likely to alter. If someone looks like an accountable person, the one is much more inclined to be a listener and follow them. However, the responsible person. Persuaders may use social resource concepts to aid in the coercion process. The first step is to achieve this.

Check out the language they use. For the Game Show example, the two quotes were identical however, the words gave them two distinct meanings. Both are incorrect. You've triggered a range of reactions. If the persuader is able to see their words as if they were things, they are able to find the right response from the person they are talking to and then oblige the person to accept the same thoughts and beliefs.

Persuaders will succeed more when they can discuss their ideas with others who are similar to themselves. This is the reason why politicians prefer to be able to unite in groups for similar ideas. If you wish to appeal to a wider audience modify your strategies to meet the needs of the new group. The cause or the other; if the person in question needs a persuasive message they will more likely to agree. There are two primary elements that affect a material agent's choice. First is physical attraction. The second is the unity factor if the person is physically attractive in this way.

The change in the attitudes of others will make it easier to obtain what you want, and you'll feel more secure. This interesting aspect has been proven to be efficient in transmitting cheap messages as well as other traits of the person being contacted like the ability to be kind, intelligent and capability. This is

Each of us contributes to increasing the chance of attractive people who are able to believe in the subject. The second aspect that is unity, is somewhat easier. The concept is that if your title is similar to an effective persuader, then you're more likely accept what the agent is looking for. This is because the method is natural and most of the time persuaders do not have to think about whether the decision is the right decision.

One method to persuade people to convince the problem to assume power. The majority of individuals believe what the experts have to say about a topic is the truth. It is more likely to seek out an expert and trusted agent on the topic. If an influencer can bring these two points into the discussion, then he has already been influenced to believe his assertion. The study was conducted to determine how this powerful method could persuade people to pay attention.

If the persuader is trying to persuade them that they are a good candidate, they should create strategies to assist them. Subjects are exposed to different types of coercion daily. Food manufacturers are trying to purchase lessons. The studio is promoting the latest blockbusters but there are also old and old movies. With all the stimulation that is available persuaders might struggle to find ways to view the object. Effective techniques have been discovered and researched. This could be extremely useful to different people many years ago. Research into these techniques began in the early 20th century. Since the purpose of persuasion involves convincing the person to make a convincing argument. If you agree with it and implement it as a fresh approach It is worthwhile to find the method that is the most effective.

Needs to be created

A way to persuade someone to alter their minds is to create new needs or address needs that are already present. If done properly, it can address the trust issue. To be successful, they have be able to address the essential requirements of the issue. Self-realization confidence, self-esteem, love food and shelter. The reason this approach is so effective for convincing is that it is actually in need of these items. It isn't something you is able to last long. If the person who persuades them believes that their business is the best or if they change their mind then they are more likely to receive more food from the shelter or even succeed.

Appeal to the social requirements of the materials. Social needs may not be as efficient as primary needs however, they are still valuable tools to utilize. People are drawn to and like being part of the group. They enjoy the kiwi ritual. Certain products may give them the impression they are part of the upper class of society. There are ideas to attract the group. The social requirements of the product can be observed in the current commercials on TV. In these commercials viewers are asked to purchase an item that makes them famous or comparable to other items.

In their efforts to persuade the social needs of the subject and desires, they can open up new areas of interest for the person. In the case of coercion, choosing the right language could make a huge difference. There are a variety of ways to say the exact same thing. One might be a proponent, however the other one does not. Make sure you use the right words and use the correct words.

If it is forced, this method is the key to success. The power of stimulation is a mind-control technique that is often undervalued. I didn't realize. It may give you more topics to choose from than other types of control over your mind. In other scenarios, the one could be forced to give up their privacy, with no control over what will happen later within the process. Concerning trust, data is presented. It is possible to make a decision even when the information is presented in the most effective possible manner and in a particular method

Chapter 9: How to use Neuro-Linguistic Programming "Manipulate" the Mind

Neuro-linguistic programming is the process of changing someone's thinking and behaviors to get the desired outcomes for them.

The fame and popularity of neuro-semantic programs also known as NLP has proven to be universal since its inception in the 1970s. Its use includes the treatment of tension and fears problem, and improves the execution of work environments or personal satisfaction.

This article will explore the theories that lies behind NLP and the evidence that supports its use in training.

What exactly is NLP?

NLP uses perceptual, behavior and correspondence strategies to assist people to modify their thinking and behaviors.

NLP relies on language preparation but should not be confused with typical language handling which has an abbreviation similar to.

NLP as an idea was proposed through John Grinder and Bander Richard who believed that it was possible to identify the reflections and actions of successful people and then to teach the others on how to apply them.

The varying interpretations of NLP makes it difficult to define. It is based by the idea that people operate on their own in-between "maps" to the outside world, which they are able to learn through touch.

NLP seeks to recognize and modify oblivious inclinations, or limitations of a person's guidebook to the world.

NLP isn't an approach to hypnotherapy. It works by the use of language in a conscious way to create changes in a person's perceptions and behavior.

One example of a central element that is a major component of NLP could be that a person is only one-sided in relation to a specific framework, also known as the most popular illustrative frame or PRS.

Advisors can detect this tendency through the use of language. Examples of this include "I can see your point" might indicate an image-related PRS. On the other hand "I understand your point" might indicate an audio-related PRS.

An NLP professional can recognize the PRS of an individual and build their restorative model around it. The system may include the building of affinity, social data affair and objective setting them.

Procedures

NLP is a broad area of training. It is true that NLP experts use a broad array of techniques that incorporate the following elements:

* Anchoring: Transforming experiences with touch into triggers to trigger certain states of passion.

*Rapports: A expert is able to detect the person by organizing their physical activities to increase their communication and response by expressing sympathy.

* A swish example: Altering the way you conduct yourself or think to reach the ideal instead of the desired outcome.

• Visual/sensation Separation (VKD) The goal is to eliminate negative ideas and emotions associated to a previous event.

NLP is used as a method to enhance self-esteem by enhancing capabilities, like self-reflection, confidence, and communication.

Specialists have used NLP economically to achieve work-related goals, such as better profitability or employment movements.

In a wider sense it is used to treat mental disorders, like anxiety, depression and tension issues. It is also known as a summed-up tension issue, also known as GAD and post-traumatic pressure issue, also known as PTSD.

The Validity

The decision of whether or not to use NLP is difficult for some reasons.

NLP isn't based on the same level of logical accuracy as established treatments, such as the psychological social treatments or CBT.

The lack of a formal guidance and the business value of NLP suggest that evidence of its efficacy are often based on stories or supplied by an NLP supplier. NLP suppliers have a financial interest in the success of NLP therefore their evidence is difficult to use.

In addition, the logical study of NLP has produced mixed results.

Certain studies have revealed benefits associated with NLP. For instance, a study published in the journal Counseling and Psychotherapy Research discovered that psychotherapy patients showed improved mental indicators and quality of life as a result of using NLP in comparison to an uncontrolled group.

An audit published within The British Journal of General Practice of 10 open investigations regarding NLP was not as positive.

There was no evidence to support the efficacy of NLP for treating well-being related issues, like tension, weight executives and substance abuse. This is due to the small amount and the nature of the study. about, rather than evidence that showed NLP did not work.

A second research survey conducted in 2015 showed NLP treatment has a positive effect on those with mental or social issues, and also because the authors said that more investigation was needed.

The theory behind NLP has also been a source of an analysis of the lack of proof-based aid.

A paper published in 2009 stated that, after three decades, the theories that underlie NLP are not conclusive, and evidence for its validity was only described.

The survey paper from 2010 sought at the results of the examination that were in line with the theories of NLP. Of the 33 investigations included only 18 percent were found to be in support of NLP's basic theories.

In this manner, despite the fact that it has been around for four years in its actuality it is not clear whether the efficacy of NLP or the validity of the theories have been demonstrated through rigorous research.

Additionally, it is important that research has generally been conducted in a positive context but there has been little research into the practicality of NLP in commercial settings.

The study of how NLP performs has some useful issues, in addition to the lack of clarity about the issue. For instance, it's difficult to conceptualize studies given the breadth of different strategies, methods and the results.

Chapter 10: Psychology Of Manipulation

Manipulation is both negative or positive. But, we would like to think that the type of manipulation we provide will help us in one way or the other. This could include enhancing our career prospects or improving our living conditions. Also, you should be aware that not all people have good intentions. Certain individuals can manipulate you in a way that leaves you feeling exhausted and wondering why the occurrence occurred. Manipulation is a psychological process. In this section, we look at the psychology behind manipulation to discover how manipulators accomplish it.

The art of controlling isn't in forcing people to do the things you want to them to do, but rather getting them to to follow what you require to get them to accomplish. One good source for reference to for this would be the Art of war by Sun Tzu. It can help you improve your confidence in this. He argues that you must be aware of your own behavior and your adversaries. How do you convince people to be compelled to do what you require to them to do? The first step is to learn about their real needs and work towards the goal you want to attain.

The closer a person will be to yours, the easier to manage. The closer an individual will be to you the easier it is to control. It is crucial to pay attention. This is why sentimental acquaintances or friends are the ideal way for testing your control capabilities. If manipulation makes you think that it's a bad word, you should consider it an influence.

It is important to convince people. You must make them believe that this was their decision right from the beginning. The majority of women need perfection, while men tend to require totality. This means that males are usually more convincing by authority and their internal self that is connected to the advancement of their lives. Therefore, displaying vulnerability about how a man might improve his personality produces the most progress. When it comes to women, being flexible to a variety of situations throughout daily life, and especially in the connection of close ones is essential. By doing this, cutting out time or affecting the relationship in a way that is not a good idea creates a longing to get it back up. All of us require a natural equilibrium at a certain point that is why we all need to give up and focus. However, statistically speaking, women tend to favor equilibrium while men focus on perfection.

Consider how you can influence the emotions of others. Because, as Maya Angelou always said, people might forget what you said or did but they'll remember the way they felt. Also, the vast majority of people need to be in control of the current moment. However, the true art of control is adoring the game of life. The key to success is perseverance. So, to understand how the experts create their "craft" appears simple it is your responsibility to create the lure feel and flow effortlessly. It will require some effort, and patience to be able to overcome your psychological barriers and set your perspective correct.

The thing that mentally harms those who control this procedure is the inability to understand and moving in the direction of nature. Similar to rock falling down the slope, you must allow gravity (nature) be in control on your. Avoid causing interfere with nature's force. When it pours down, we can adjust with an umbrella or a coat. If it gets hot then we shift our fashion to lighter layers of clothing due to the heat. The basic idea is to not be rigid, and adjust according to the rules of. What is the best way to measure the illusion? Two different methods: making the right decision when faced with the case of an insensitive request is an unsuitable thing, also known as, misprioritization of needs and desires to yield from an unsuitable piece of information. In order to understand people, it is important to be aware of their personality as well as how they react to certain situations and also what are their limitations.

This is the best part. The mental structures that are causing the problems are off track. How do you help them to achieve the goal? First of all you must be the one to lead by demonstrating the benefits. The people love the reward. How can be the "thing" you require to accomplish yield a profit? Don't inform them that they are legally required that they must do it. Research has shown that most of the time, people hate the idea of being able to decide what to do. Instead, you aid them in achieving the same conclusion on your own "way". People love the feeling that they made the decision (not the thought of you). Therefore, let them have the feeling. The primary part is to attach to the "reward" or benefit to the item. If people don't understand what benefits they can gain from something then they'll probably not take it on.

Also, take a close examine the connections between what those who do the things you're trying to teach in the absence of an additional "thing". In the case of, for instance, you have to convince someone to become more fit, proposing the notion of a "diet" is difficult. Try to discuss better skin structure, which is, in turn, linked to a dazzling diet regimen.

It is possible to lead people to the source of their water However, every now and again it isn't possible to make them drink. In the end, however you need to make them feel thirsty. It's all about the interest! Bring the person interested in subjects and you'll have nature's help like a stone sliding down a slope due to gravity. Do not ignore every law of logic and simply follow it. If you've succeeded in manipulating, don't reveal yourself because it can be difficult to ignore your adoring and loving nature and others are likely to cut off your communication. It's not necessary. Be aware of how you make people feel and try to influence them, "convince", generally positive, don't be malicious.

How to Keep Track of Manipulators

A lot of times you might be manipulated into noticing the manipulators. In their mind, it is their intention that you recognize them in order to achieve their goal of manipulating your thoughts. However, I've conducted research and observed the tactics manipulators employ to use to avoid being observed. However, it is essential to be aware of these techniques when your privileges or interests as well as health are in doubt.

It is the Physical Space Advantages

A manipulative person might demand your attention and invite you to an actual room where the individual in question is able to exercise more control and strength. This could be in the control's workplace, house, automobile or other spaces in which the person feels a sense of belonging and security (and in the event that you require to be).

It gives you the chance to speak first to establish Your Basis and Identify weaknesses

A lot of sales reps use this technique when they meet with you. In asking you general looking at questions and gathering an understanding of your thinking and behavior. From this, they will be capable of assessing your abilities and flaws. This kind of questioning using a hidden motive can also be observed in the workplace or even in home relationships.

Control of the Facts

It involves lying, rational making, deceitfulness, and punishing the victim for causing their suffering. Also, it involves deformity of the truth, vital disclosure or retention of crucial information, distortion, a modest portrayal of the truth and an inequitable disposition of the issues.

Make You astonished with facts and Statistics

Some people enjoy "scholarly torture" by pretending to become the master and best in particular regions. They abuse you by imposing false claims about certainties, measurements as well as other data you consider to be a bit naive. This is often the case in financial transactions and deals as well as in expert dialogs and negotiations, and also in social and political disputes. When you assume control of you, the person in charge will try to make their motives to the maximum extent possible. Certain people employ this method without a reason, other except to experience a sense of predominance in scholarly research.

Beware of Methods and Red Tape

Certain people utilize organization desk procedures, methods such as laws and by-laws advisory groups, and other routes to preserve their power and position but also making life difficult. The system could also be used to delay the process of searching and truth seeking or shroud imperfections and flaws and avoid the need for examination.

Roaring Their Voices and Displaying Negative Emotions

Some people are more vocal in public conversations to show a sense of control that is forceful. The possibility is that in the event that they think they'll speak in a way that is loud enough, or express unhappiness, you'll yield to their pressure and offer them what they require. The powerful voice is most often coupled with strong non-verbal signals like using energized or standing signals to increase the sway.

Negative Surprises

Certain people employ counter surprise to shake you and improve your mental position. It could range from being a low ball in an exchange, to an unexpected call which the person doesn't have the choice of coming through and communicate in some way or in another way. In most cases, the alarming negative information is delivered abruptly and you are given an opportunity to be prepared and prepare to counter the situation. The controller could request additional concessions from you in order to continue in contact with.

Giving You Very Little or No Time at All to Decide

This is a standard arrangement and deal-making strategy where the person in charge demands you to make a decision prior to you being. By putting pressure and control over the subject, it is expected by the controller that you'll "split" and comply with the demands of the attacker.

Negative Humor Intended to Poke at Your Limitations and Depower You

Some controllers prefer to make small-scale remarks, usually disguised as jokes or humour in order to make you appear less than and less secured. Models may include a variety of comments ranging from your appearance, the more sophisticated model on your cell phone to expertise and credentials, all the way to how you walked in a hurry and exhausted. In order to make you look bad and making you feel uncomfortable, the perpetrator will try to assert mental dominance over you.

Do not be afraid to criticize and judge you to Make You Feel Bad

In contrast to the previous conduct in which negative cleverness was used as a way to spread out and the control freak in and out, singles out you. In the constant process of overestimating, mocking, and denying the person you are, she makes you feel a bit numb and keeps the dominance of her. The person who is in control creates the perception that there's always an issue in you, and regardless of the effort you try, you're inadequate and never adequate. In the end, the attacker focuses on the negative, without offering genuine and beneficial solutions or offering concrete methods to assist.

The Silent Treatment

By deliberately not responding to your calls and messages, instant messages, or any other requests, the system assumes control by causing you to pause and thereby causing the impression of vulnerability and uncertainty in your brain. The silent treatment is a brain game in which silence is used as a method of influence.

Imagine Ignorance

This is an excellent "playing foolish" method. If you think that your child isn't aware of what you want or what you require to accomplish the forceful/controller forces you to accept the responsibility and makes you begin sweating. A handful of kids use this technique to delay of their actions, to slow them down, and force adults to do their own tasks that they would prefer not to accomplish. Adults may employ this method also when they have an issue to hide or commit to keep an appropriate distance from.

Blame Baiting

It is comprised of excessive accusation of the weaknesses of the beneficiary, and focusing on an additional factor that could be responsible to the controller's happiness and success or discontent and sorrow. Focusing on the person's passion for failures and weaknesses the controller entraps the beneficiary to give up on absurd demands and demands.

Victimhood

Models: Overblown or envisioned individual problems. Medical problems that are not properly represented or imagined. Reliance. Codependency. A deliberate act of fragility that evokes sympathy and provide support. It is a game of being weak, weak or saintly. The motive behind manipulative victimhood tends to be to abuse the victim's powerful willpower, guilt or obligation, commitment, or to use defensive and supporting feelings, in order to gain unintentional advantages and concessions.

Manipulative Relationships

Although you may be more familiar with the most frequent factors that lead to a relationship being unhappy like an ex-partner who pressures you to wear something or hinders your ability to be social with your family and friends There are many more indicators that indicate your relationship is obsessed, manipulative, or unhealthful. Read the article and be sure to trust your instincts and don't let anyone communicate with you using the way they think it will make sense for you. It should be a pleasant experience and not overwhelming, scary or exhausting. Having your partner help you feel better and not make you feel sadder.

The Signs You Need to Pay Attention to in a relationship that is emotionally abusive

If you're in a relationship with a toxic person often, you will not be aware. Instead, those around you know the relationship is not good. It is because love could have blinded you to the fact that you're not aware of the warning signs. Here are some things to look for when examining an abusive and manipulative relationship.

You feel guilty when you Spend time with friends

When we imagine someone trying to remove their loved one from their emotional support network in the majority of cases, we portion imagine something dazzling that is similar to the detestable spouse. However, all things taken into consideration, controlling partners generally cut you off from your intimate family in a more subtle way.

In contrast to slyly preventing your loved ones or familymembers, the controlling partner could gently force you to leave them. They can make you feel extremely uncomfortable about having that is not in the relationship. Most people don't want about these feelings therefore, you could change your behaviour and where you go or who you are with, etc. It is important to avoid being remorseful. First of all, it makes you feel like your partner is really in love with you, so it's easy not to recognize that something is taking place, particularly in the case of a history of being treated in as such as a child.

Perhaps your partner is grumpy every time you have a night out with your closest friends until you decide to avoid the weekend and lunch dates in order to avoid the stress. Maybe your spouse or husband is a negative person towards your buddies until you start to realize that their reactions are true. Maybe your activities in public revolve around an activity you enjoy you enjoy but your new spouse thinks that your hobby is a joke and calls you stupid. They ridicule you until you decide to end it. This behavior can be encapsulated in many forms but it usually is a common goal of severing or cutting off the relationships with people that you have a connection with until you realize that you are the most important person on earth.

Chapter 11: Deception Tactics

Everybody knows that when deceit is discussed, there is typically a negative motive behind it. Deception is an important part of psychology that is dark. A lot of people have been successful in converting lying and deceit, but they are both distinct. It is true that lying is a type of deceit, but deceit is not a lie in and of itself. Instead of defining deceit as lies, it's more appropriate to view it as an act that is misleading. Any act that has the potential of convincing someone as true in the event that it's not, can be classified as deceit.

Deceptions can be described as offering evidence to support a falsehood and lying, or implying falsehood , or concealing the truth. However, not all instances that deceive are a sign of dark psychological practices. In a certain degree, all uses deceit in at some point or the other. Certain people are able to deceive others for a variety of motives like feeling inadequacy, embarrassment , or sincerity. Research has shown that the majority of males are inclined to make up their height on dating sites. Of course, this doesn't mean that they're engaging in dark psychological practices. Dark psychology is far more serious than the other. Certain people even commit false claims about their happiness, health, and even their ambitions. These types of deceit aren't comparable to the dark psychology kind of deceit.

The deceit can be dark if it is done using a negative image and completely disregard for the feelings of the person who is being misled. People who employ the dark psychology employ the deceit with the sole intention to hurt their victims not to aid them. They are doing it for the sake of their own interests regardless of the person who suffers by the act.

Many people believe that small-scale deceptions can't be considered to be dark, whereas large-scale deceits are nothing more than dark. They are wildly wrong. It's not the size or the weight of the deceit that decides if deceit can be described as dark, instead, it's the motive behind the deceit which determines its degree of darkness.

Deception In The Spectrum Of Deception

Distributed deception platforms have evolved way beyond honeypot trapping strategies and are specifically designed to provide high-interaction deceptions, early detection and study of attacks' lateral movements. Furthermore, deception platforms alter the attack's asymmetry by giving security personnel an advantage when threats enter their network, thereby forcing attackers to be correct 100 percent of the time or be recognized as well as by providing decoys that obscure the attack's surface, and by providing important counterintelligence and threat intelligence which is needed to defeat the human attacker with advanced capabilities.

Small deceptions are often used in a devious and powerful manner by a master manipulator and the result can be much more brutal in comparison to larger-scale forms of deceit. Small deceptions are usually used to determine the level of trustworthiness and to induce them to believe in the deceitful words as well as the actions taken by the manipulator. If the victim is conditioned in the hands of the manipulator in a number of smaller lies and deceptions, they are more likely to be influenced by larger falsehoods in time.

Small deceits can also be used to undermine the victim's faith in their ability to use logic. If a manipulator attempts to fool a victim through small deceptions , and the victim starts to doubt the truth and concludes that their suspicions are incorrect and they are unable to doubt their own judgement. People are more likely to believe that their judgement is incorrect than someone else fooling them about less important matters. The vicious victims of dark psychology are aware of the trust that people have , and they benefit from it, without mercy or consideration for the well-being of the victim.

In the larger scale, deceit could also be a sure clue to the dark side of psychology. One of the techniques that have worked for years is convincing another that you're a distinct person from what they claim you are. This isn't about your personality or behaviour. In this case, you're talking about your whole identity. Your name, birth date, if you can even your sex! The most skilled user of dark psychology usually tries to convince people of their fake identity and background.

The money element is usually the source of deceit since deception and money have crossed paths numerous occasions in recent times. Some people use deceit to gain cash while others use deceit to hide their own wealth or their lack of. Because money is a popular subject in the realm of deceit, a handful of its deceitful ways of using it will be investigated.

The most well-known deceits of dark psychology that involve money is displayed by beggars. These aren't the typical street begging; these beggars are attempting to steal money from people, even having plenty. These beggars employ a range of dark psychological techniques to extort cash of innocent people. Beggars of this kind do not hesitate to inflict harm on themselves to appear more desperate the victims. These deceivers have been found to use their family members as part of this kind of fraud and make their children drug addicts to employ them to commit fraud. It is impossible to quantify the extent of deceitful financial practices.

Another area where deceit is used is that the issue of marriage status. Many people conceal their marital background with the intent of wooing the new victim. It could be in order to make money or get sexual pleasure, or any other motives that are known only to the person manipulating. Some men have several wives scattered across the globe, however the wives don't know each other's names. This type of deceit but, it is now more difficult due to the rise of the internet that gives individuals the chance to check into other profiles through social media. The most successful deceivers, regardless of internet, have managed to masterfully conceal their tracks, and keep their fake wife from each others successfully.

Additionally, there are individuals who appear to be married, but in reality, they're not. This kind of fraud is possible due to various reasons. The couple that is married is generally believed to be the couple is still waiting to be tied. There are those who lie about getting married due to the fact that they're seeking methods to evade tax or receive insurance benefits. Another deceit in this respect is to make up the deceased spouse or husband to gain sympathy of the public and, in most cases the income as a consequence.

Many people make up lies about their criminal record. This is because it's almost impossible to trust anyone in a professional or personal capacity in the event that you're discovered to be a former convict. One example is where a woman comes across someone who's committed a grave criminal act during the course of his life. It is usually not the norm for the man to divulge his past to a woman in the hope that the woman will be forced to end their relationship when they learn the truth. It is interesting that this kind of defiantness to disclose one's previous criminal history is not connected to dark psychology. However, if the man hides the truth for the goal of hurting his partner in the future, then this fraud is considered to be as dark.

They often believe that deceit is a great way to hide the flaws they display. It prevents their victims from being aware of what kind of person they really are until the harm is already done. For instance, if someone who is using dark psychology is interested in a person to have sex, they are aware that the focus of their attention will signal a warning for the person they are targeting, therefore they'll try to use the trick. They might be lying or convince the victim to realize that their motive is love and devotion. The victim is eventually enticed by the deceit and when the manipulator is able to get what they want, they throw away the wounded victim like an unclean piece of cloth and then moves on to an intriguing targets.

Deception allows you to implement solutions for detecting the threat and responding. This is vital in the current era with staffing shortages. Deception does not just enhance defenses by providing early and accurate engagement-based detection , but it can also play a crucial role in preventing attacks by providing visibility tools that can identify likely routes of attack, time-lapsed maps of movement of attackers and integrations to speed up incident response.

While cyberattacks are growing in both sophistication and quantity Deception-based technology offers precise, reliable detection and response to network threats. Businesses are increasingly resorting to deception in order to reduce the gap in detection and gain an edge over adversaries by allowing them to carry out counterintelligence, boost their expenses, and reduce their attacks.

It is usually the most preferred method of deceit. It is used whenever manipulators find the victims of their manipulation are susceptible to lies and are not able to see the truth. It could be that the victim is generally a confident person, or because the manipulator has cautiously worked on their victims for a long time, until they lose their guard. Most skilled manipulators have a way to get around every strategy they attempt to implement They usually have an "Plan B" whenever they use their dark deceit.

The deceitful use of lies is typically executed to the very last detail. A skilled deceiver will try to blend their lies and the truth in a manner that it is difficult to separate the lies from the truth. A manipulator could tell an untruth that is 90 percent accurate and 10 percent false. The victim will view the truth as 100% accurate and will have no ways to differentiate the lie from the truth since they're blended precisely.

Implying is a less obvious type of falsehood than outright lying. Implying means expressing the idea the possibility that something that is not true instead of stating it with conviction. If someone wishes to deceive someone regarding the amount of money they own, they can either lie or make up. The lie could be something such as "I have been extremely successful. I've made a lot in money" but the manipulator realizes that this isn't being the reality. However, the statement might be something like "It's extremely difficult to work for my tax accountant. The effort to reduce my tax bill consumes lots of my time". In this way the manipulator has behaved in a manner that suggests they are wealthy , without explicitly declaring that they don't have two cents to rub together.

There are many deception options available, ranging from simple traps, and fully-automated deception systems. Although individual deceptions have advantages when used in conjunction with other methods This article will focus on the characteristics common to the deception systems that are distributed in the market, which are sought after due to their extensive detection and reaction to the most advanced threats.

In essence, deception is designed to identify attackers when they conduct reconnaissance further from the compromised system, or when they attempt to steal credentials from different systems. The assumption behind deceit is that no one should ever be using decoys, deception servers, baits, or lures because they do not provide production capability that employees can have access to. The assets of deception aren't promoted to employees, and any attempt to identify them is a red alert and any involvement should be prompted by immediate action to stop attackers from increasing their intrusion.

The technology of deception plays a key function in changing the nature of attacks. But, in order for deception to succeed you must have credibility and attractiveness to deceive skilled human attackers. Active Directory credential verification authenticates fraudulent credentials for attractive target. The fake operating systems and allows adaptation to match the environment of production can appear authentic and fool hackers into disclosing their presence. Facades based on emulation can be detected quickly and easily avoided by attackers. Techniques for behavioral deception that are dynamic enhance deception using machine learning that adjusts to the behaviour that the networks display, the applications as well as device profiles. It constantly refreshes itself to stay attractive.

Furthermore adaptive deception permits organizations to reset their deception network at any time. If you are concerned about attacks resetting the attack's attack surface will prevent fingerprinting by attackers, which can be used to identify and disarm decoys, generate uncertainty and increase the probability that an attacker will make mistakes. The added complexity and expense of restarting could slow down the attack process and act as a deterrent, causing the attacker to re-start or find a more suitable attack target.

The Deception-Based Detection system is intended to catch attacks on networks earlier, regardless of attack method. Contrary to other types of detection, this method doesn't require time to master the network, and can be effective when it is deployed. The endpoint, network and application, as well as data as well as Active Directory deceptions work collectively to spot lateral movements and credential theft, man-in the-middle efforts, as well as Active Directory attacks.

The threats and attack surfaces are constantly changing and detection techniques must be able to adapt to ensure an early warning of threats both at the point of entry, and in the course of their movement through the network. Deception technologies that are comprehensive scale to change in the attack surface and detects threats across the user network, remote office/branch offices and data centers and also supports data migration to cloud, as well as special networks like point-of-sale systems. Out-of-band deployments are the most effective for effectiveness and scalability for operations and agentless deception of endpoints makes deployment easier and easier to manage. If your business employs an endpoint-based detection system search for vendors that have integrations that allow for automated deployment options and integrated management.

Deception systems that incorporate threat analysis for attack will help in the analysis and correlating of indicators of compromised information that can be utilized to speed up incident response. Forensic evidence and threat intelligence reports let companies track and document every attack's activity to aid in an understanding of the motives of the attacker which could lead to more secure overall. Deception solutions are able to detect attacker behavior and, through integrations, communicate the entire tactics, strategies and methods of interactions with firewalls security and event-management systems as well as network access control software and endpoint devices. These integrations also enable automated blocks and isolation for compromised devices.

By using files which contain fake sensitive information and beaconing technology which calls back when an attacker tries to access it Counterintelligence can be obtained about which kinds of files were stolen , as well as an understanding of where the data goes.

Deception can slow the attack down as attackers get caught up in the illusion area even though they believe they are ramping up their attacks. The use of adaptive deception adds difficulty for the attacker through changing dynamically the attack surface for attackers, thereby increasing their costs and being an deterrent. In addition, the ability to obscure the attack surface has been demonstrated by pen testers who have also been a victim to deception and were tracked for days only to be defeated.

Furthermore that, the high-interaction deception used by ransomware could slow an attack by up to 25% or so. The drives that are deceived can entice hackers and supply them with massive amounts of fake data in order to keep them entertained while the affected system is disconnected from the internet.

The manipulators usually choose to consider the implications since they offer them the possibility of plausible denial. If the victim claims that the manipulator is not telling the truth, then they is able to claim that they didn't lie and that they are technically correct.

The absence is a deliberate decision to not mention anything that is truthful or significant. This is distinct from other deceptions such as lies and implications because they use lies to cover up the truth. It is simply not acknowledging the truth , and directing to the person being victimized away or offering the victim the opportunity to inquire about the subject of the omission. One way in which omission can be used is to create the appearance of an "emotional fence" surrounding a specific scenario. This is the time when experienced manipulators say certain periods that they have lived through, as well as even situations they encounter are not suitable to think about. The discussion of them could reveal old wounds that they've tried to treat. The victim, feeling empathy for the person who deceived them, will try to avoid discussing it.

Fraud is thought to be the most shady form of deceit used by people who use dark psychological techniques. Imagine fraud as being like a lie that is based on steroids. Instead of blaming things that have happened in their past A dark deceiver might use fake documents or tales, as well as other evidence to justify their claims. But, they do it in a different way however. They don't rant about their accomplishments in the way that the fake documents have shown, but they place the documents in strategically placed places in the hopes that their target is likely to find them. They are aware that if they seem overly insistent in their claims, the victim may suspect there's something amiss, that they're not lying. The suspect victim could start their own investigation of the manipulator with being aware of the receiver.

Today even fraud has become among the more popular types of deceit due to the advent of computers and internet connectivity. People who manipulate can make use of professional grade software to quickly and effortlessly create realistic-looking documents of any kind. These kinds of frauds are carried out to satisfy personal or professional motives. An example of this is one where individuals have been able get jobs using a fake identitydocuments, which were stolen from a business, and then vanished before their identity could be identified. Personal fraud is also a part of frightening stories like those of people suffering from HIV spread the disease through the aid of fraudulently issued documents of good sexual health.

In relationships, deceit can lead to feelings of suspicion and distrust between the lovers. Many people expect their loved ones, family members, or friends to be honest every day When trust is damaged because of deceit the result is typically difficult to recover the feeling of trust.

Chapter 12: Learn To Understand the 4 Personality Qualities In The Dark Triad

Narcissism

A person who is regarded as a narcissist will exhibit a variety of characteristics that they exhibit. They may have an overly exaggerated self-worth, for example thinking that their lives are exceptional and is among the top significant lives of all time. If they have been overinflated enough, they could conclude that they are the most significant person in the world.

In the eyes of a narcissist aren't just unique however, they are above everybody else. They think they are an elite person, superior to the normal human beings. Since a narcissist thinks that way, their actions are likely to alter. The behavior you see in a narcissist is likely reflect the self-worth person.

The most obvious indicators or signs of this condition include the inability to tolerate any form of dissent and criticisms of all type. Even if they think somebody is trying to criticize their character, they're likely be unable to handling this. The person who is this has a need to see others support their opinions all the time, and likes to be delighted. If you're around those who appear to require constant praise, acknowledgement and appreciation and also if they appear to plan their lives to ensure they have access to those who satisfy this desire and satisfy this need, then it's likely you're working with an egotist.

Three of these aspects are expected to combine to create what is known as the Dark Triad. If a person has all three of these traits in them, it could be challenging to remain clear from whatever plans they might are involved in. Be aware of these three traits could make a significant difference in the amount of control you have over your own life.

We refer to a desire for grandness, a perpetual desire for approval and admiration and a feeling of superiority, as well as the feeling of being exceptional and a willingness to be open to criticism that leads to the search for situations and people who provide praise and acknowledgement.

The fantasies of its total strength and its immense sense of importance are two of the most prevalent traits of narcissists in the majority. The majority of them are the ones to blame for the endless applause they received as children while talking about their fantasies. When they are adults, these individuals will continue to require the love of everywhere because they've created the notion that their coworkers are the most important people in the world.

The sense of self-worth that is internalized by narcissists affects their external appearance. This is usually evident in two ways: agreement and praise, criticism or a dislike of dismissal. Consensus and lobbying are oxygen for the ego of the narcissist while criticism and discord can be compared to poison. Imagine an inherited dictatorship to appreciate how narcissism is perceived when it reaches its ultimate conclusion. They demand the worship of the people who are in charge as well as the creation of a memorial, and total obedience and respect. Every act of disagreement will quickly and severely be punished. North Korea would be an ideal modern illustration of the extreme manifestation of Narcissism. The rulers of this nation seek to be revered as Gods and repress anyone who dares to voice an opinion or an idea that isn't completely in line with the state doctrine.

Machiavellianism

The characteristics of this character include a desire to keep a focus on your own interests always as well as an awareness of the importance of your appearance and the way you perceive your appearance, and the brutal exercise of cruelty and power instead of having compassion or mercy.

For simplicity People who possess this characteristic always have a plan for how they take on life. The consequences, as well as any implications of every action have be thought through and then evaluated by the ways they'll influence the person taking them. The Machiavellian method of looking at the world can be summarized by asking the following question: "How will this action help me? And how will my public image be affected as a result?"

Machiavellian people will be the masters of things that will personal benefit them and yet be capable of maintaining the positive public image they wish to have. This lets the manipulator do what they wantto do, and yet still allowing those around them to admire them.

Instead, it reveals manipulative skills as well as high rationality and the ability to plan every specifics of movements until they justify even the most ineffective methods or morally deficient methods. exploiting others and circumstances to gain advantage.

For many who do not fit the strict definition of Machiavellianism Their government figures typically reflect their true self. Everyone alters their appearance and public behavior slightly however, in the end the majority of people's exterior appearance is nothing more than a polished representation of the person they are. They usually have a clear notion of who they actually and the person they portray before the world. The most notable example is the case of serial murderers. The best of them have often avoided the reach of the law due to their appearance is closest to their obsession with death. One of the most famous examples is the one of the serial killer Ted Bundy. According to the people who knew Ted Bundy, he was a gorgeous person. He also spoke very well and showed that no one believed that he was carrying one bone that was not within his body. He was able to kill more than 30 females before being eventually captured.

There are many instances of this difference between the intention and the appearance in less severe fields like serial murder can be found. There are many tales of business leaders who have succeeded in brutally cutting down on employment and maximizing profits at the maximum level. In terms of Machiavellianism the best leaders can get people to accept that they are driven to do so, or are even compassionate! These rulers can be considered the role models for people who just want to fulfill their own desires but also seem to be 'a member of the masses. One of the traits for Machiavellian men is their ability to take advantage of people. Let's take a look at one example to see this clearly. An individual who has just joined an office with Machiavellian features would see every coworker and boss or team member as a resource , or piece of a larger puzzle to make use of and utilize. The Machiavellian wouldn't see the other members of the team as human beings but instead see them as a collection of threats to the organization's strategic plan and weaknesses to control, exploit or counter. This is one of the main reasons of the reason why Machiavellians have become so aware of the way they act. They realize that their outward appearance is essential to effectively use effect and profit every person they encounter.

Another aspect of the Machiavellians was the creation of fear into their surroundings. This is a direct result of The Prince's story, which encourages people to be terrified and loved at the simultaneously. If this isn't feasible, the book says that those who are afraid are more likely to love. However the notion of loving and fear is directly linked to the Machiavellian ability to distinguish between the perception of private and public. The ideal Machiavellian could create fear and even obedience in those who appear to be feeling more feelings of love over fear.

Psychopathy

Psychopathy is characterised by the lack or lack of sympathy, insignificant sense of remorse and guilt and anxiety in regard towards the negative consequences of an reckless and unjust actions and lack of interest in the various areas of one's actions and difficulties in communicating emotions and feelings which can lead to lack of empathy.

The term refers to a mental condition which is characterised by shallow charm, an impulsivity and a deficiency of the human emotions we are accustomed to like remorse or empathy. Anyone who displays enough of these characteristics can be classified as psychopath. They are considered to be one of the most dangerous types of people due to the fact that they can conceal their motives, but creating a lot of problems.

The word "psychopath" in terms that someone is insane and who wields machetes. But the reality is different and this makes it more dangerous. A psychopath who is truly dangerous is much more likely the attractive and beautiful stranger who can convince their victims before destroying their victims and their lives.

It is interesting to note that many of the most successful businesspeople score well on tests for psychopathy. As time passes the trend is becoming more prevalent to think of psychopathy as an issue for the victim and the society, rather than a problem within the individual's life. Psychopaths can rise the top of whatever that they want to because they don't need to be concerned about the pity-indecisions others encounter.

The three distinct characteristics that make up the Dark personality can cause it to take on significant traits in regards to character and behavior. Particularly, the person who has The Dark Triad tends to be manipulative to the point of exploitation others for his or his or her own benefit, with an indifferent and cold outlook to the results of their actions and a constant musing of right and grandeur, which drives his or her actions.

In the realm of emotions In the emotional sphere, he is attracted by strong feelings across a variety of areas, leading to the point of performing dangerous and extreme acts on behalf of others or himself with no concern, guilt or moral sanity. He is extremely concerned about his appearance and self-image and is meticulous about his appearance and a lack of concern for critiques from outside that are seen as evidence of someone else lack of capacity and inexperience and resulting in the severing of relationships that are influenced by the circumstances.

But, they're generally attractive and smart enough to think about their actions well and on time.

In every way it is crucial to know how this group of people are manifesting themselves to be able to recognize them early and be able to defend themselves against their dangers. Charm is among the most typical behaviors of psychopaths. Charm is a characteristic that should be considered as superficial, not genuine, real charm. If you imagine someone who was truly charming in your life, you're likely to know that they have positive traits that are able to support their external actions. If a person is truly charming to show kindness and kindness, they should not be labelled as a psychopath. Psychopaths are able to display all the exterior signs of charm, such as the physical appeal, obvious warmth and an interest in other people. The motive behind these flags is the reason why they are so bright red. As a part in a formula, psychopaths can see the appeal. The manipulator will often inquire whether the charm causes the victim the feeling of a certain emotion in a particular way and also if the result is positive or beneficial. They are rational people who are dependent on normal human emotions. It is also a characteristic that distinguishes psychopaths. We all lie every day. It doesn't mean that we are all psychopaths. However, when paired with other traits, it may be a sign of a psychotic personality. The act of lying is as normal for psychopaths as breathing for the majority of people who are mentally healthy. A psychopath is able to present their reality convincingly in a specific moment, as it is what it has to be. Psychopaths also do not exhibit signs of lying because they don't feel any emotions or feelings of resentment or guilt over their deceit. Psychopaths believe that lying is simply doing what's necessary at the moment.'

A lack of control over impulses is a different characteristic of psychopathy. Many people have processes and internal controls to stop them from acting in a hurry. The prevention mechanisms are not in place for psychopaths. If a psychopath spots an opportunity to make use of it, they will do it without hesitation, or even a second thought. This could involve killing someone they wish to kill, or robbing somebody, or even stealing items they wish to take. This impulsiveness and cruelty is what makes psychopaths among the most successful individuals in different fields including the military and business. Automated execution of a critical action is something that non-psychopaths don't have and it can be detrimental to the lives of others.

The lack of remorse is another thing that differentiates psychopaths as opposed to nonpsychopaths. Many who have committed an act of violence, like murder, are utterly accountable for what they've committed and have taken their own life because of these emotions. Psychopaths do not choose to be regretful. They can't perform the act physically. The idea of asking a psychopath to feel guilt is similar to asking a deaf person play music. A lack of guilt is directly connected to a lack of guilt. Most people feel guilt when they breach an ethical standard They value themselves. Because psychopaths think in a different way or in a way that is correct, they consider what is useful or unimportant; their guilt is an entirely different notion. The closest thing to psychopaths' guilt or regret is the fact that he did not conduct his psychopathic actions in accordance to its higher standards.

Conclusion

Utilizing persuasion and manipulation techniques can assist us in improving various areas of our life. There is a dark side and mystery that surrounds this subject when we think about the way that mind control is utilized in extreme ways.

When you're aware of the reasons behind employing these methods, we can start to enhance our lives. It's not the technique that is good or evil, however the person who employs these methods. Perhaps you've learned to become effective in your work or with your friends. However, whatever your motives are, you can take this on with an unshakeable conscience and everything will be fine. If you do it in the right manner, everyone wins.